Break Free to Own Your Space

Speak with Confidence and Reclaim Your Boundaries

MG Lazarus

Break Free to Own Your Space
Speak with Confidence and Reclaim Your Boundaries

Self-Published

Copyright © 2024 by MG Lazarus

All rights reserved. No part of this book may be reproduced, stored in a retrieval system, or transmitted in any form or by any means—electronic, mechanical, photocopying, recording, or otherwise—without the publisher's prior written permission.

Location: Republic of Ireland

Disclaimer:

The stories in this book are based on real experiences, though some fictitious elements have been included to illustrate key concepts clearly. To protect the privacy of clients, all names used in these stories are pseudonyms.

Website: https://proventherapy.com/

Email: mg@proventherapy.com

DEDICATION

To my family, friends, and colleagues—thank you for being my teachers in the art of assertiveness.
Through every conversation, challenge, and moment of growth, you've shaped my voice and strengthened my resolve.
This journey is dedicated to you.

Acknowledgments

I thank You, Lord, for walking before me, showing the way, and lighting my path. Your strength and grace have been my constant guide throughout this journey.

To my family, friends, and colleagues—thank you for your love, wisdom, honesty, and the countless conversations that shaped this work. Many of you have been my teachers, inspiring and enriching the lessons that culminated in this book.

I extend my heartfelt gratitude to Dr. Michele Brannigan, Clinical Director and Consultant Psychiatrist. Your unwavering support and encouragement have been a beacon of strength to me.

To my esteemed colleague and friend, Teresa Dunphy, Senior Clinical Psychologist—your insightful feedback and guidance in refining the psychological concepts presented here have been truly invaluable.

To all the HSE (Ireland) Mental Health Teams I have had the privilege of working with—thank you for your support, critical comments, and encouragement. Your impact on my journey has been profound and deeply appreciated.

With deepest appreciation to all who have walked this path with me—thank you for being a part of this journey and for imparting lessons that words can scarcely capture.

About this book

If you're feeling worn out from constantly saying "yes" to keep the peace, you're not alone—and it doesn't have to be this way. *Break Free to Own Your Space* is a guide to reclaiming your voice and setting boundaries that respect your needs. This book isn't just about learning to say "no" but about building a healthier, more confident relationship with yourself.

Through relatable stories, practical tools, and simple exercises, this book offers real support on your journey. Here's what you'll find:

- **Down-to-Earth Tools to Build Assertiveness**: With exercises rooted in Cognitive Behavioral Therapy (CBT), like reframing negative thoughts and using "I" statements, you'll get hands-on guidance to start speaking up in ways that feel natural.

- **Everyday Stories You Can See Yourself In**: Read about others who, just like you, found themselves trapped in people-pleasing patterns—and took steps to break free. Their stories offer encouragement and practical examples to learn from.

- **Strategies for Boundaries That Feel Right**: Get tips on how to express your needs clearly, kindly, and confidently so you can handle challenging situations at work, with friends, and even with family.

- **Confidence-Boosting Techniques**: Identify the thoughts that keep you second-guessing yourself and discover ways to shift them. You'll build self-confidence that feels genuine—not forced.

Whether you're taking the first steps to overcome people-pleasing or already working on assertiveness, *Break Free to Own Your Space* gives you the tools, insights, and encouragement to start living life on your terms. You'll walk away with practical skills and a renewed sense of self-worth.

Table of Contents

Acknowledgments iv

About this book v

Discovering Your Inner Voice 10

   From People-Pleaser to Assertive Communicator 10

   The Art of Assertiveness – the   Professional Way 16

From Silence to Strength 19

   Why Assertiveness? 19

   What Is Assertiveness? 21

   How Is It Different? 23

   Identifying Thought Distortions 24

   Sarah's Story 33

Are You Truly Assertive? 40

   Identifying Your Assertiveness Level 43

   Real-Life Incident: Mark's Reflection 45

Starting Strong! 54

   Building Self-Esteem and Confidence 55

   Understanding Your Rights and Responsibilities 61

   The Role of Body Language 63

   Emily's Transformation 70

Speak Your Truth! 78

- "I" Statements and Active Listening 79
- Refusal Techniques 86
- How to Express Feelings and Needs Clearly 89
- John's Promotion Request 91

When Sparks Fly 98
- From Silence to Self-Respect 98
- Strategies for Negotiation and Compromise 105
- Look at that mirror; don't break it! 109

Making Your Mark 116
- Finding Her Voice: Jane's Story 116
- Assertiveness at Workplace 121
- Setting Professional Boundaries 124
- Dealing with Difficult Colleagues 129
- When Cultural Norms Collide: My Story 133
- Speak Up or Miss Out: Alex's Promotion Story 135

Bridging Hearts and Boundaries 141
- Maintaining Relationships While Being Assertive 142
- Emma's Overcommitment to Her Friend 145
- Balancing Assertiveness and Empathy 151
- Julia's Family Gathering 154

Breaking Free 161
- Facing Common Fears and Moving Past Them 162
- Dealing with Setbacks 165

    Maintaining Assertiveness Under Pressure 167

    Tom's Boardroom Challenge: Learning to Speak Up . 171

Own Your Journey! 176

    Reflecting on What You've Learned 178

    Continuing Your Journey: Embracing Growth 180

    Moving Forward with Confidence 183

Appendices 188

    Appendix 1: Daily Interaction Log Template 188

    Appendix 2: Mental Rehearsal Script 190

    Appendix 3: Achievements Log Template 193

    Appendix 4: Practical Conversation Starters 194

    Appendix 5: Refusal Phrases 198

    Appendix 6: Examples of "I" Statements 201

    Appendix 7: Daily Thought Log 204

    Appendix 8: Examples of Constructive Feedback 207

    Appendix 9: Confident Communication 210

    Appendix 10: Bibliography 212

    Appendix 11: Glossary of Terms 214

About the Author 218

Introduction

Discovering Your Inner Voice

"Assertiveness is not what you do, it's who you are." — *Shakti Gawain*

From People-Pleaser to Assertive Communicator

I was a people-pleaser. Sounds harmless enough, right? However, as I learned over time, it was an attitude that I had to change for everyone's good. It was a painful journey that inspired the creation of this book, an accomplished fact.

Let me explain.

Working in a team of professionals was far more challenging than I initially expected. As the only male from a different ethnic and cultural background, I quickly became the odd one out in this particular team, and unfortunately, I was treated as such.

In many instances, I found myself facing behavior that felt both dismissive and isolating. There were subtle yet pointed actions—like the avoidance of eye contact during discussions or sarcastic remarks that left me feeling diminished. These weren't isolated events, and over time, they created a sense of being marginalized. The impact on me was significant, leading to feelings of alienation and unfair treatment. What made it even more disheartening was the setting—this was a team dedicated to fostering respect, inclusion, and dignity. The contrast between the mission and reality was a stark one I couldn't ignore.

In my attempt to avoid conflicts, disagreements, and unwelcoming gestures, I leaned into my people-pleasing tendencies. I thought that being agreeable could smooth over tensions and create a less stressful work environment.

So, what did I do?

When someone made a comment to undermine me or when someone completely ignored me in a group conversation, I'd put on a naïve face, pretending not to understand the insult. But this approach came with a cost. The more I avoided addressing these slights, the more emboldened the bullies became.

My silence was their green light, and it only fueled their behavior further.

As a Senior on the team, I wasn't under their direct line of management, and there was no clear governance or accountability structure to protect me during those days. However, the excessive scrutiny and attempts to undermine me intensified until I reached a breaking point. It became clearer that if I didn't address the problem head-on, it would only continue—and likely get worse.

But how?

I realized that I must work on this.

Where will I start? I had no idea!

My mind was clouded, and I was still perambulating all over the place without having some definite plan!

It took some time for me to finally reach out to the therapy toolkits to find a starting point.

Yet another realization!

When it comes to helping others as a therapist, I will have an answer, but when I wanted to help myself, I wasn't thinking about my therapy skills and readily available tools!

The first thing I had to do was to tame my rising thoughts, the hyperactive, challenging, and oppositional mind, to calm it down. I tried to slow down by reassuring myself that this would also pass; it was a positive affirmation!

Cognitive restructuring was my next step as I realized that much of my thoughts were unduly 'catastrophizing!' The rest of the story is the reason behind this book.

In absolute summary, here are the assertive strategies that I applied to turn things around:

1. **Be genuine and authentic**: I had to drop the artificially created naïve façade. Pretending not to understand the insults only encouraged more bullying. I learned that being authentic in my responses was crucial.

2. **Give constructive feedback**: I started giving direct feedback to those who undermined me. This wasn't about confrontation; it was about calmly and clearly addressing the behavior and how it impacted me. (For practical examples on how to address undermining behavior constructively, see Appendix 8: Examples of Constructive Feedback for Undermining Behavior.)

3. **Show dissent confidently and politely**: I began to express my dissent confidently but politely. It's possible to disagree without being disagreeable, and I made sure that my tone and words reflected that balance. For example, a statement of this kind did help in my case, "I see where you're coming from, and I'd like to offer a different perspective. Here's how I view it…"

4. **Communicate next steps**: Finally, I made it clear that I knew the next steps I could take and wasn't hesitant to take them if necessary. It wasn't a threat but rather a message to them that I was informed, prepared, and willing to act if the behavior continued. This may sound difficult. So, I am giving some example statements in Appendix 9: Confident Communication.

This was a significant learning curve for me. I realized that if you don't address a problem, you're not just allowing it to continue—you're giving it permission to grow. Through this experience, I transitioned from being a people-pleaser to an assertive communicator, and it's a journey that I hope can inspire and guide others facing similar challenges.

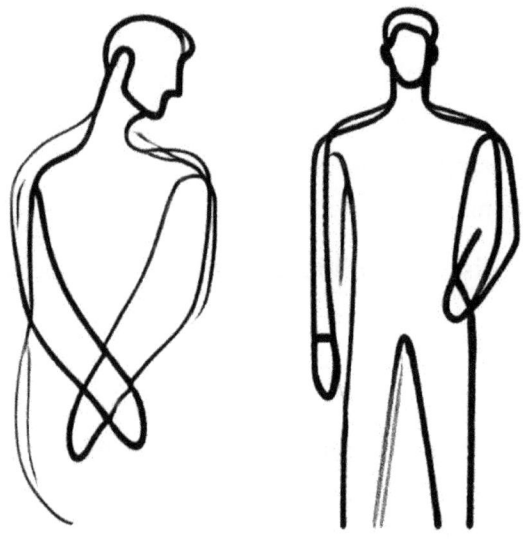

From Vulnerability to Strength: The Power of Assertiveness

Over the years in my career in mental health, I had the chance to work with a variety of teams, each bringing its own set of challenges and dynamics. As I moved from one team to the next, something stood out to me: the kind of treatment I faced in those early days, when assertiveness was still a struggle for me, never resurfaced.

Reflecting on this, it's clear that developing my assertive communication skills was a game-changer. By the time I joined those later teams, I had learned how to stand my ground, how to set boundaries that protected my well-being, and how to communicate my needs openly and honestly. This wasn't just about avoiding conflict; it was about transforming the way I interacted with others.

I was no longer an easy target for those who might have sought to bully or manipulate me. Instead, I was able to connect with my colleagues on equal terms, fostering mutual respect and understanding.

Assertiveness became my shield, but it was also much more than that. It empowered me to play a more meaningful role within the team, lead confidently, and handle the ups and downs of workplace dynamics with a steady hand.

After stepping out of the shadows of people-pleasing, I understood just how crucial assertiveness is in our personal and professional lives. This journey taught me an invaluable lesson: while we can't always dictate how others behave, we can absolutely choose how we respond. And when that response is assertive—when it's rooted in clarity, confidence, and respect—we don't just safeguard our own sense of self but contribute to creating a work environment that's healthier, more respectful, and more supportive for everyone involved.

In the pages ahead, we'll explore how you can cultivate this quality in your own life. You'll learn the practical skills needed to communicate assertively, and you'll see how this approach can enhance your relationships, reduce stress, and help you deal with life's challenges with confidence and grace.

Whether you're naturally reserved or more outspoken, there's a place for assertiveness in your life—and this book will show you how to find it.

The Art of Assertiveness – the Professional Way

Assertiveness is an art, especially in a professional setting where the balance between confidence and respect is crucial.

The techniques and insights we'll explore are designed to help you build your assertive skills in a way that's both impactful and gentle. You'll learn how to navigate professional interactions with confidence, ensuring that your voice is heard without creating tension or discomfort.

Whether you're leading a team, collaborating with colleagues, or communicating with clients, assertiveness allows you to express your ideas and needs clearly while maintaining positive, respectful relationships. It's not about pushing others aside or forcing your way through—it's about standing firm in your own space while still valuing the perspectives and feelings of those around you.

This book will guide you through the process of integrating assertiveness into your professional life in a way that feels natural and empowering. By the end, you'll have the tools to enhance your career and your personal well-being, all while fostering an environment of mutual respect and understanding.

A Personal Story

Let me share a quick story with you. Early in his career, John encountered a significant challenge. He was handed a project that he knew would overwhelm his already packed schedule, but he felt pressured to say yes.

The decision weighed heavily on John, affecting both his work performance and his personal life. However, with the guidance of counseling, John learned to assert his needs and stand up for his rights. This moment marked a turning point in his life and made him realize just how crucial assertiveness is.

Learning to say "no" isn't about rejecting opportunities; it's about protecting your space, time, and priorities. Whether you're facing a difficult boss, a demanding family member, or simply trying to juggle the many hats you wear every day, assertiveness is your key to doing it all with grace.

This is a journey worth taking. Whether you're looking to break free from people-pleasing, like I did, or simply want to improve how you communicate, this book is your guide to becoming a more assertive, confident, and fulfilled individual.

Each chapter will build on the last as we move forward, helping you understand and master assertiveness. You'll learn to recognize when you're not being assertive and how to adjust your behavior. You'll practice through exercises and reflect on your interactions.

So, let's begin this transformative journey towards mastering the art of assertiveness and enhancing your conversations and connections with others.

Chapter 1

From Silence to Strength

Unleashing the Power of Assertiveness

"Dare to stand up for yourself, dare to be who you are." — Maya Angelou

Why Assertiveness?

Imagine you're in a therapy session, working through why you feel constantly overwhelmed and confused. You feel a familiar weight in your chest, as some thoughts have been bothering and confusing you for some time.

Could I really say 'no' without feeling guilty?

What if saying no makes me seem selfish?

What if they think I don't care?

What if they get upset and stop including me?

Am I being too harsh by setting boundaries?

As you talk with your therapist, it becomes clear that the real issue isn't the workload or the people around you—it's your struggle to say "no," to draw a line, to assert your own needs.

What to expect: In this chapter, you'll explore what

assertiveness truly means and why it's a cornerstone of healthy communication. We'll define assertiveness and how it differs from passive and aggressive behaviors, helping you discover that assertiveness isn't about conflict—it's about respect. By the end of this chapter, you'll understand why assertiveness is empowering and foundational to personal and professional well-being.

In today's world, where personal and professional lives often blur together, the pressure to conform is overwhelming. Many people, myself included, have fallen into the trap of thinking we must keep our heads down and our voices quiet to maintain peace.

But what happens when you do this?

- You lose yourself!
- You sacrifice your own needs and desires to make others happy.
- You may be seen as shy, unintelligent, uncompetitive, or not smart enough.
- This will eventually disturb your self-image, potentially affecting your mental health and general well-being.

Assertiveness is the antidote to this.

It's not about being a bulldozer, steamrolling over others to get what you want.

It's quite the opposite.

True assertiveness is about clarity and respect—respect for yourself and those around you. It's about speaking up when it matters, stating your needs, desires, and limits confidently, and doing so in a way that leaves room for others to do the same.

In my sessions with clients, I observe how their minds create negative thoughts as if they would antagonize or displease others by saying 'no.' It takes some time for them to understand that being assertive isn't just about avoiding conflict—it's about taking back control of their lives. They eventually start setting boundaries, saying "no" when needed, and expressing their thoughts without fear of judgment.

And you know what?

They start to feel better, more grounded, and more at peace.

What Is Assertiveness?

In a world where we're often encouraged to either push too hard or stay too quiet, assertiveness strikes the perfect balance. It's about saying, "This is what I think," or "This is what I need," and doing so in a way that's clear, confident, and considerate.

People often associate assertiveness with being bold, stubborn, or aggressive. Some see it as loud, shouting, or demanding dominance. On the other hand, assertiveness is the quality of being self-assured and confident without crossing the line into aggression. Being assertive ensures that your thoughts and needs are heard and respected.

Assertiveness is a communication style, but it's also so much more than that. It's a mindset, a way of interacting with the world that prioritizes honesty, clarity, and mutual respect. When you're assertive, you express your feelings, thoughts, beliefs, and needs directly and honestly.

There's no beating around the bush, no sugar-coating, and no silence when something needs to be said. But here's the key: you do it all with respect—for yourself and others.

Being assertive isn't about winning or losing. It's about standing on equal ground with others, where everyone's voice has value. It means you respect your own needs and ideas enough to bring them to the table, and you respect others enough to listen to theirs.

Are you okay to give it a try? Do this mental rehearsal now.

Imagine you're in a supportive and safe environment, like a counseling room, and you're finally ready to talk about something that's been bothering you for weeks. Maybe it's an issue at work or a recurring conflict with a loved one. Being assertive in that moment means you don't hold back, but you also don't lash out. You state your case clearly, you express how you feel, and you do it in a way that opens the door to understanding rather than slamming it shut with anger or resentment. (A helpful tool is included in Appendix 2: Mental Rehearsal Script for Practicing Assertiveness).

How Is It Different?

Assertiveness is not just a communication skill; it's a way of life that allows you to express yourself confidently and comfortably. Refer to the table below to compare what assertiveness is and what it is not.

Aspect	What Assertiveness Is	What It Is Not
Expression of Needs	Expressing your needs clearly and directly.	Being aggressive or confrontational.
Respect for Rights	Respecting both your own and others' rights.	Ignoring the needs or feelings of others.
Confidence in Communication	Communicating with confidence.	Dominating or overpowering others.
Active Listening	Listening actively and responding appropriately.	Manipulating or guilt-tripping others.
Boundary Setting	Setting and maintaining healthy boundaries.	Being passive or avoiding conflict.
Saying "No"	Saying "no" when necessary without guilt.	Saying "yes" to avoid displeasing others.
Self-Expression	Using "I" statements to convey your feelings.	Blaming or accusing others.
Solution-Seeking	Seeking win-win solutions.	Insisting on having things your way.
Emotional Control	Remaining calm and composed.	Letting emotions dictate your responses.
Standing Up for Yourself	Standing up for yourself respectfully.	Allowing others to walk all over you.

In my work with clients, I often see the transformative power of assertiveness. When someone learns to express themselves assertively, they're no longer afraid to ask for what they need or to say "no" when it's necessary. They learn that it's possible to be firm without being harsh and to be strong without being unkind. They start to see that assertiveness isn't just a way of communicating—it's a way of living that honors both their own worth and the worth of those around them.

Reflective Question: When was the last time you felt unheard in a conversation? How did it make you feel?

Identifying Thought Distortions

Let's dive into some theory now. This is good to know. Trust me, I won't make you bored!

People-pleasing behaviors are difficult to change because they often arise from automatic, unhelpful thoughts, a process known as cognitive chaining. These thoughts can become ingrained, influencing our self-perception, relationships, and even our sense of self-worth.

Let me clarify in simple terms. See the following thoughts:

If I say no, they'll be disappointed in me.

If I don't agree, they might take it personally or think I don't care.

I should go along with this to avoid conflict.

If I assert myself, they'll think I'm difficult to work with.

It's better to stay quiet than risk upsetting someone.

It is easier to just go along than to stir up any trouble.

Sounds familiar? Then, you're likely dealing with thought distortions.

In Cognitive Behavioral Therapy (CBT), thought distortions refer to patterns of thinking that can exaggerate our fears or make situations feel more daunting than they are. Below are some common thought distortions that fuel people-pleasing and hold us back from being assertive.

If you think this is getting too theoretical, don't worry; you will get the idea very soon:

1. **Mind Reading**: Assuming you know what others are thinking. For example, you might think, "They'll see me as selfish if I turn down their request." Are you sure of this? Do you have some evidence? 'No' is the answer. But you believe they will see you as selfish if you reject their request!

2. **Catastrophizing**: Believing that the worst possible outcome will happen. To explore this, I usually ask, "What could be the worst thing to happen if you turn down their request?" The answer will be something similar to, "If I assert myself, they'll never speak to me again." One client told me, "They will reject me." Again, there's no evidence for this because, while doing reality testing, it clarified that this anticipated consequence hadn't happened before!

3. **Personalization**: Taking responsibility for things that aren't yours to own. For example, "If they're upset, it must be my fault," or, "If I don't agree, it'll ruin the group dynamic." Any evidence? Absolutely nothing!

4. **Should Statements**: Telling yourself you "should"

do things in a certain way to keep the peace or avoid judgment. Thoughts like, "I should always be agreeable," reinforce people-pleasing by imposing unnecessary rules on yourself.

By identifying these thought distortions, you can start challenging them and replace them with more balanced, assertive beliefs.

Exercise: Challenging Thought Distortions

Here's a simple exercise to help you identify and rethink thought distortions that might be holding you back:

1. **Notice your thoughts**: The next time you feel pressured to say "yes" when you want to say "no," pause and ask yourself what thoughts are going through your mind. Write them down if you can.

2. **Identify the distortion**: Check if any of these thoughts fit a typical distortion pattern (exaggerated consequences or fears). For instance, are you assuming you know what someone else is thinking? Are you catastrophizing the outcome?

3. **Challenge and reframe**: Ask yourself if there's real evidence for this thought. What might be a more balanced perspective? For example, instead of thinking, "They'll hate me if I say no," try to reframe it as, "They might be disappointed, but that doesn't mean they'll think less of me as a person."

Example: Reframing a People-Pleasing Thought

Imagine you're asked to take on extra work that you don't have the capacity for. Your initial thought might be, "If I say no, they'll think I'm not committed." Here's how you could challenge and reframe it:

- **Original Thought**: "If I say no, they'll think I'm not committed."
- **Identified Distortion**: Mind Reading. You're assuming you know how they'll interpret your response.
- **Balanced Thought**: "It's okay to set limits, and saying no won't make me less committed. In fact, saying no, at this time, will help me deliver better quality work on my current projects."

By practicing this reframing process, you'll develop a more assertive mindset, making it easier to respond authentically without feeling overwhelmed by distorted thoughts.

This technique is powerful for anyone learning to set boundaries, as it shifts focus from ungrounded fears to realistic, empowering perspectives. Thought distortions can keep us locked in people-pleasing cycles, but by recognizing and challenging them, you begin the process of reclaiming your voice and standing tall in your truth.

Refer to the table below to discover the benefits of being assertive and standing up for yourself.

Aspect	People-Pleasing	Benefits of Assertiveness
Boundaries	Struggles to say "no," leading to overcommitment and burnout.	Sets and maintains healthy boundaries, protecting personal time and energy.
Self-Respect	Often sacrifices own needs and self-worth to please others.	Increases self-respect by valuing personal needs and opinions.
Stress Levels	Prone to high stress and anxiety due to unexpressed feelings and needs.	Reduces stress by enabling open and honest communication.
Interpersonal Respect	Vulnerable to being taken advantage of or overlooked by others.	Gains respect from others, making it less likely to be manipulated or disregarded.
Communication Clarity	May lead to miscommunication and misunderstandings by avoiding conflict.	Enhances communication by ensuring clear expression of thoughts and needs.
Emotional Energy	Often experiences emotional exhaustion from prioritizing others' needs.	Fosters balanced relationships, where mutual respect and understanding are prioritized.

By embracing assertiveness, you're not just learning to avoid conflict—you're learning to respect yourself and your needs. You're learning to communicate in a way that's honest, clear, and fair.

What Does It Mean to Be Assertive?

We've touched on the idea that being assertive means communicating your thoughts, needs, and feelings directly and respectfully. We also discussed the psychology behind our people-pleasing approach, which is mainly caused by our thought distortions. Let's now dive a bit deeper into what assertiveness truly involves.

At its core, assertiveness is about balance. It's about finding that sweet spot between passivity and aggression—where you can express yourself openly and honestly without stepping on anyone else's toes. When you're assertive, you're standing up for your own rights while simultaneously respecting the rights of others.

Imagine being in a conversation where you need to voice a concern or set a boundary. An assertive approach, as already discussed, would mean expressing your thoughts clearly, without hesitation or sugar-coating, but also without anger or hostility. It's not about demanding your way but rather about making sure your voice is heard, and your needs are acknowledged while remaining considerate of the other person's feelings and perspectives.

Assertiveness empowers you to engage in exchanges that are honest and open, free from resentment or guilt. You're able to say what you mean without feeling bad about it later and without causing unnecessary friction. This kind of communication builds trust and respect in your relationships—whether at work, at home, or in any other area of your life.

When you practice assertiveness, you're not just speaking up; you're fostering a sense of mutual understanding and respect. You're showing others that you value your own needs and ideas just as much as you value theirs. And in doing so, you're creating an environment where everyone feels more comfortable and confident in expressing themselves.

In the end, being assertive is about more than just communication—it's about living authentically and maintaining self-respect while also honoring the dignity of those around you. It's a skill that enhances your interactions, strengthens your relationships, and contributes to a more fulfilling, balanced life.

Distinguishing Between Assertiveness, Aggressiveness, and Passivity

When it comes to communication, understanding the differences between assertiveness, aggressiveness, and passivity is essential for building respectful and productive relationships. Each style has a unique impact on how your needs are expressed and how you engage with others. The goal is to strike a balance, communicating in a way that respects both your own needs and the perspectives of those around you.

Here's a closer look at each style, along with examples to illustrate their effects.

1. **Assertive Communication:** You advocate for yourself while considering others' viewpoints. Example: "I understand your point, and here's another perspective."

2. **Aggressive Communication:** You push your agenda irrespective of others' feelings. Example: "This is the only correct way!"

3. **Passive Communication:** You suppress your own needs and desires. Example: Staying silent even when you disagree.

Aspect	Assertiveness	Aggressiveness	Passivity
Expression	Clearly communicates thoughts, needs, and feelings with respect for all parties.	Forces one's viewpoint with little regard for others' needs.	Avoids expressing needs or opinions, often yielding to others.
Respect for Others	Balances self-respect with respect for others' boundaries.	Disregards others' boundaries, aiming to dominate.	Overlooks personal needs to keep the peace, often disregarding self-respect.
Communication Tone	Uses calm, confident language without blaming or demanding.	Tends to be confrontational, loud, or hostile.	Often speaks softly or with hesitation, suggesting insecurity.
Conflict Handling	Seeks solutions that consider both parties' needs and perspectives.	Pushes for win-lose outcomes, often creating further conflict.	Avoids conflict altogether, leading to unresolved issues.
Personal Boundaries	Sets clear boundaries and maintains them respectfully.	Ignores others' boundaries to impose personal needs or desires.	Lacks boundaries, often saying "yes" to avoid conflict or please others.
Emotional Impact	Reduces stress and fosters mutual respect.	Increases tension and potential resentment from others.	Leads to frustration, resentment, and lower self-worth over time.

Reflective Question: Think of a time you responded aggressively or passively. What might have changed if you had responded assertively?

Here are some possible responses people might give in real life about the impact of responding assertively instead of aggressively or passively.

1. **From Passive to Assertive:**

    - "If I had spoken up about my preferences instead of just going along with what everyone else wanted, I think I would have enjoyed myself more and felt respected. It would have shown them that my opinions are also valuable."

2. **From Aggressive to Assertive:**

    - "Instead of yelling and getting angry when my colleague missed the deadline, if I had calmly discussed the impact of their actions on the team and asked how we could avoid this in the future, it might have preserved our relationship and led to a more constructive solution."

3. **From Passive to Assertive:**

    - "When I didn't tell my friend that I was upset about them constantly canceling our plans, nothing changed. If I had been more assertive, perhaps they would have understood how their actions affected me, and it might have improved our communication and respect for each other's time."

4. **From Aggressive to Assertive:**

    - "Reacting aggressively when I was incorrectly charged for an item in the store made the situation tense and the staff defensive. If I had approached the situation more assertively and politely pointed out the error, the correction might have been handled more smoothly and pleasantly."

5. **From Passive to Assertive:**

    - "I always let my partner decide our weekend plans. If I were more assertive about my own preferences, we might have a more balanced relationship where both our interests are considered, making our time together more enjoyable for both of us."

6. **From Aggressive to Assertive:**

    - "I got into a shouting match with a neighbor over parking. If I had been more assertive and less confrontational, we could have possibly come to a mutual agreement without causing hard feelings that lasted for weeks."

These responses highlight how switching from a passive or aggressive response to an assertive one could lead to more positive outcomes, enhancing relationships, reducing conflict, and promoting mutual respect.

Sarah's Story

Let me tell you about Sarah, a project manager who faced a common challenge in the workplace. Sarah was known for her kindness and easygoing nature, but her aversion to confrontation often came at a cost. She found it difficult to push back or set firm boundaries with her team, which led to missed deadlines and a growing sense of frustration, both for her and for those she worked with.

Sarah knew she needed to step in but hesitated. *What if they think I'm too demanding?* she worried, her mind spinning with potential reactions. *But if I don't set expectations, we'll keep missing deadlines.*

Sarah's reluctance to assert herself meant that her team often took liberties with deadlines, focusing on creative ideas without considering the constraints of time. While innovation was never an issue, meeting project goals on time was. The tension between nurturing creativity and maintaining discipline was something Sarah struggled with daily.

Things changed when Sarah attended a workshop on assertiveness. The workshop opened her eyes to the power of clear, direct communication. She learned that assertiveness wasn't about being harsh or controlling—it was about being clear and firm, setting expectations, and ensuring that everyone was on the same page.

Armed with these new skills, Sarah approached her next team meeting differently. With confidence, she addressed the group, saying, "I really appreciate all the creative ideas everyone is bringing to the table, but we need to refocus on meeting our initial deadlines." This wasn't just a statement; it was a turning point. Her team responded positively, recognizing the importance of balancing creativity with accountability.

The shift was almost immediate. With Sarah's clear and assertive leadership, the team met their deadlines, and the project was completed on time. But the benefits went beyond just meeting one deadline—this change in Sarah's approach had a ripple effect on her career. Her ability to lead assertively improved her team's performance, earned her respect, and positioned her as a more decisive, more effective leader within the organization.

Sarah's story is a powerful reminder that assertiveness isn't about shutting down others' ideas or being inflexible. It's about guiding the team with clarity, setting expectations that everyone understands, and creating an environment where creativity and discipline coexist. In learning to be assertive, Sarah not only enhanced her own career but also fostered a more productive, collaborative team dynamic.

Reflective Question: Have you ever avoided confrontation to keep the peace and protect your people-pleaser image? What was the outcome?

Recap: Embracing Assertiveness

As we wrap up Chapter 1, it's clear that assertiveness is much more than just a communication skill—it's a vital tool for living a balanced and fulfilling life. Throughout this chapter, we've explored the foundational aspects of what it means to be assertive, highlighting the importance of respecting both your own needs and the needs of others.

Assertiveness empowers you to navigate life's challenges with confidence and grace. It allows you to communicate your thoughts, needs, and feelings openly, without fear of judgment or conflict. By setting clear boundaries and expressing yourself honestly, you're not just protecting your own well-being—you're also fostering healthier, more respectful relationships with those around you.

Remember, the journey to becoming more assertive is just beginning. The insights and reflections from this chapter are the first steps toward transforming how you interact with the world. As you move forward, keep these key takeaways in mind:

- **Assertiveness is about balance**: It's not about being aggressive or passive but finding a middle ground where you can express yourself clearly and respectfully.

- **Communication is key**: Being assertive helps you communicate more effectively, reducing misunderstandings and building stronger connections.

- **Respect is mutual**: When you practice assertiveness, you honor your own rights while also respecting the rights of others.

As we continue through the next chapters, you'll gain practical tools and strategies to further develop your assertiveness in both personal and professional settings.

So, take a moment to reflect on what you've learned so far. How has your understanding of assertiveness evolved? What steps will you take to start integrating these principles into your daily life?

The path to assertiveness is a journey—one that leads to greater self-respect, improved relationships, and a more empowered you. Let's continue this journey together.

In Practice: Key Steps to Begin Understanding Assertiveness

1. **Recognize your communication style**

   Reflect on how you typically respond in interactions. Are you more passive, aggressive, or assertive?

Recognizing your style is the first step to making meaningful changes.

2. **Understand what assertiveness means**

   Remember that assertiveness is about balance—expressing your needs, thoughts, and feelings clearly while respecting others. It's not about controlling or avoiding but finding that respectful middle ground.

3. **Identify the benefits of assertiveness**

   Remind yourself of the positive changes assertiveness can bring: reduced stress, stronger relationships, and a greater sense of self-respect. Each time you practice being assertive, you take steps toward these benefits.

4. **Start practicing "I" statements**

   Practice framing your thoughts using "I" statements (e.g., "I feel...," "I need...") to focus on your experience rather than placing blame. This technique can help you express yourself clearly and minimize defensiveness in others. We will discuss more in the following chapters.

5. **Set small, realistic goals**

   Begin with simple situations where you can practice being more assertive, like saying no to minor requests or expressing a small preference. These small steps will build your confidence over time.

6. **Observe and reflect**

   After practicing assertiveness, take a moment to reflect on the experience. How did it feel? How did others respond? Use each experience as a learning tool to refine your approach.

   Applying these steps in small ways will make you more comfortable with assertive communication. Building assertiveness is a journey—take it one interaction at a time!

Chapter 2:

Are You Truly Assertive?

A Self-Discovery Guide

"Knowing yourself is the beginning of all wisdom." — Aristotle

To embark on the journey toward becoming more assertive, it's crucial to understand where you currently stand in your communication style. Before you can make meaningful changes, you need a clear picture of your natural tendencies—whether you lean toward assertiveness, passivity, or aggression.

What to Expect: This chapter guides you through a self-assessment, helping you identify your natural communication style—whether assertive, passive, or aggressive. Through exercises and reflective questions, you'll gain insights into your behavior patterns and set a baseline for personal growth. Understanding where you stand is the first step to meaningful change.

Are you someone who often says "yes" when you really want to say "no"? Do you struggle to voice your opinions for fear of causing conflict? Or perhaps you find yourself being more forceful than intended when trying to get your point across?

Understanding your current style is the first and

most important step toward growth. By recognizing your strengths and identifying areas for improvement, you'll be better equipped to make the changes necessary to become more assertive. This chapter will provide you with the tools to assess your communication style honestly and constructively, setting the stage for the transformative journey ahead.

Remember, self-assessment isn't about labeling yourself or finding fault with yourself. It's about gaining insight into your behavior so you can build on what's working and address what's not. As you move through these exercises, keep an open mind and be kind to yourself.

As someone rightly said in the past, 'awareness is cure,' growth begins with self-awareness, and this chapter is your starting point on the path to more confident and effective communication.

Look at this question: How do you typically respond when someone cuts in line in front of you?

When asked how they typically respond to someone cutting in line, people's answers vary widely depending on their personalities, cultural backgrounds, and assertive skills. Here are a few possible answers people might give in real life to this reflective question:

1. **Avoidance**: "I usually don't say anything because I want to avoid confrontation. It's not worth the hassle."

2. **Passive Aggression**: "I might sigh loudly or make a sarcastic comment loud enough for them to hear, but I won't directly confront them."

3. **Direct and Polite**: "I usually call their attention and politely let them know there's a line that they skipped."

4. **Assertive**: "I calmly explain that we've all been waiting in line and ask them to join at the back."

5. **Aggressive**: "I tell them off right there and make sure they know it's not okay to cut in line."

6. **Indifference**: "It doesn't really bother me. I just let it go because there are more important things to worry about."

7. **Humor**: "I might crack a joke about it to lighten the mood, but I'll make sure the message is clear that they need to go to the back."

Each of these responses offers insight into different ways people handle situations where they might feel infringed upon but have various levels of comfort with confrontation.

Can you re-read the question above and write down your answer on a sheet of paper for your own self-reflection?

Identifying Your Assertiveness Level

Our communication styles can shift depending on the situation, who we're talking to, and how we're feeling in the moment. Sometimes, you might find yourself staying quiet to avoid conflict, while other times, you might speak more forcefully than intended. It's natural for these behaviors to fluctuate, but understanding your dominant communication style is the first step toward becoming more assertive.

Do you tend to hold back your thoughts, or do you sometimes push too hard to get your point across? Or maybe you already balance things well, expressing yourself with both confidence and respect.

As mentioned, it isn't about labeling yourself or putting yourself in a box. It's about getting clear on your tendencies so you can make small, meaningful adjustments. By knowing your predominant style, you can start to communicate more effectively, no matter the situation.

As you go through the questions below, take a moment to reflect on your usual Yes or No responses. Be honest with yourself—this is a tool for growth. The insights you gain here will help you build on your strengths and work on areas that could use a little improvement as you continue to develop your assertiveness skills.

1. Do you find it difficult to say no to unreasonable requests?

2. Do you often find yourself apologizing, even when you believe you are not at fault?

3. Do you express your needs and opinions even when they are unpopular?

Your answers can reveal a lot about your assertiveness:

- Mostly saying 'yes' and making unnecessary apologies indicate a passive style.

- A tendency to impose your views could suggest an aggressive style.

- Comfortably expressing your needs typically signifies assertiveness.

Reflective Question: Can you recall a recent interaction that demonstrates your usual communication style? How do you feel about it?

Real-Life Incident: Mark's Reflection

Mark was the kind of person everyone described as easy-going. He was a team player who never hesitated to take on extra tasks, and his willingness to help made him well-liked by his colleagues. But there was a downside to Mark's accommodating nature. Over time, he found himself buried under a mountain of work, constantly juggling multiple projects and struggling to keep up. Despite his best efforts, the weight of these responsibilities began to take a toll on him physically and mentally.

Mark had always thought of his easy-going attitude as a strength, a way to avoid conflict and keep the peace. But after feeling increasingly overwhelmed and burnt out, he began to realize that something wasn't right.

One late evening, as Mark sat at his desk, he looked around the empty office and sighed. *Why am I always the one staying late?* He wondered, exhaustion settling heavily on him. *I can't keep saying "yes" just to keep everyone happy.* He realized he'd been prioritizing others' needs over his own well-being, fearing that a "no" would disrupt the harmony he valued so much.

During a self-assessment exercise, he took a hard

look at his habits and patterns. That's when it hit him—his inability to say "no" was more than just a personality trait; it was a sign that he was leaning toward passivity rather than assertiveness.

This realization was a turning point for Mark. He understood that while being helpful was a positive quality, it had become a double-edged sword. His tendency to take on too much was not just harming his productivity but also his overall well-being. Motivated by this insight, Mark decided it was time to make a change.

He sought advice on how to set boundaries and

began practicing small, deliberate steps to be more assertive. Instead of immediately agreeing to every request, he started to evaluate his capacity and respond accordingly. He learned to say "no" when he needed to, without feeling guilty or fearing that it would upset others.

The impact of these changes was profound. By setting clear boundaries, Mark regained control over his workload and found a healthier balance between his professional responsibilities and personal life. Not only did his stress levels decrease, but his job satisfaction improved significantly. Mark discovered that by being more assertive, he could still be the easy-going person his colleagues valued—only now, he was also someone who knew how to protect his time and energy.

Mark's journey is a powerful reminder that assertiveness isn't about being difficult or refusing to help others. It's about understanding your own limits and ensuring that you're not sacrificing your well-being for the sake of others. In the end, Mark became not just a better colleague but a happier and more fulfilled individual.

Automatic Thought Record: Tracking Your Assertive Moments

One powerful tool for building self-awareness in assertive communication is an **Automatic Thought Record (ATR)**. In CBT, ATRs help people understand their automatic thoughts in specific situations and how those thoughts influence their emotions and actions. By tracking your responses to situations where you might struggle with assertiveness, you'll begin to notice recurring patterns and gain the insight needed to start reshaping them.

Often, the thoughts that hold you back from being assertive are automatic; they spring up instantly. An ATR can help slow down that process by making those thoughts more visible. For example, you might realize that every time you're asked to take on extra work, you think, "I can't say no because they'll be disappointed." The ATR will help you recognize these moments and reframe your responses.

Exercise: Keeping an Automatic Thought Record

Here's how to use an ATR to track interactions where you feel challenged to be assertive. Aim to complete this exercise for at least a week to gain insights into your natural responses.

1. **Situation**: Describe the scenario that triggered your response. Be specific—include where it happened, who was involved, and what was asked of you.

2. **Automatic Thought**: Write down the first thought that popped into your mind. Was it a worry about disappointing someone? A fear of rejection? Record the exact words you thought.

3. **Emotion**: Note how this thought made you feel. Were you anxious, guilty, or maybe frustrated? Rating the intensity of your emotion on a scale of 1–10 can help you see which situations affect you the most.

4. **Response**: Write down what you did in response to the thought. Did you agree to something you didn't want to do? Did you stay silent even though you had something to say?

5. **Alternative Thought**: Now, consider how you could reframe this thought in a more balanced way. For example, instead of thinking, "They'll think I'm selfish if I say no," you could try, "It's okay to set limits; saying no doesn't make me a bad person."

6. **New Response**: Imagine how you might act if you held the alternative thought. Would you set a boundary, ask for clarification, or calmly express your needs?

Example of an Automatic Thought Record

Let's look at a sample ATR to see how this works in practice.

- **Situation**: My manager asked me to take on an extra project with a tight deadline.

- **Automatic Thought**: "If I say no, they'll think I'm not committed."

- **Emotion**: Anxious (8/10 on anxiety scale)

- **Response**: I said yes, even though I'm already overwhelmed with other tasks.

- **Alternative Thought**: "I can explain my current workload and ask if there's a way to prioritize or redistribute tasks."

- **New Response**: Politely tell my manager that I'm at full capacity and ask if someone else could take on the project or if another task could be deprioritized.

By filling out the ATR regularly, you'll start to see patterns emerge—such as specific thoughts that frequently prevent you from asserting yourself. This awareness can be the first step to creating new responses that align with your goals for assertive, healthy communication. Over time, the ATR exercise will make it easier to catch yourself in the moment, giving you the opportunity to pause, reframe, and respond assertively.

To build awareness of your responses over time, use the Daily Thought Log in Appendix 7. This tool helps you track patterns in your thoughts and actions, guiding you to replace unhelpful thoughts with balanced, assertive ones. Recording these daily experiences can strengthen your confidence and help you see your progress.

Exercises to Recognize Your Communication Style

1. Daily Interaction Log (use the template in Appendix 1 at the end of this book): Record key interactions where you expressed a need or handled a disagreement for one week. Note your approach and how you felt about the interaction.

2. Role-Playing: With a friend or mentor, practice scenarios where you need to be assertive. This can help highlight your natural inclinations and areas for improvement.

Reflective Question: What patterns do you notice in your interaction log?

Recap

As we conclude Chapter 2, it's important to recognize the value of understanding where you currently stand in terms of assertiveness. Just like any journey, knowing your starting point is essential if you want to reach your destination. The exercises in this chapter were not just about identifying whether you're more passive, aggressive, or assertive—they were about building self-awareness, the cornerstone of personal growth.

By taking the time to reflect on your communication habits, you've laid the groundwork for meaningful change. You've started to uncover the patterns that shape your interactions, and with this insight, you're better equipped to make conscious choices that align with your goals. Whether you've discovered a tendency to hold back, push too hard, or strike a balance, this awareness is the first step toward becoming more assertive in a way that feels authentic to you.

As we move forward into the next chapters, you'll find more detailed strategies and techniques designed to help you enhance your assertiveness. But remember, the work you've done here is crucial. It's the foundation upon which these strategies will build. With a clear understanding of your baseline, you're now prepared to delve deeper into the practical tools that will empower you to communicate more effectively and confidently.

Let's carry this momentum into the next chapter, where we'll explore actionable techniques to further develop your assertiveness and apply it in real-life situations.

Reflective Question: What is one change you can make today to become more assertive in your interactions?

In Practice: Key Steps for Self-Assessment

1. **Identify your dominant communication style**

    Reflect on recent interactions. Do you find yourself leaning towards passivity, aggressiveness, or assertiveness? Knowing your natural tendencies provides a baseline for growth.

2. **Track patterns with a daily interaction log**

    Use the template in Appendix 1 to record key interactions over the next week. Note how you responded to each situation and how you felt afterward. This practice helps you recognize patterns in your communication.

3. **Reflect on situational changes**

    Observe if your communication style changes depending on the person or setting. For example, do you communicate assertively with friends but feel more passive at work? Recognizing these shifts can highlight areas for targeted improvement.

4. **Ask yourself reflective questions**

    Use the reflective questions in this chapter to deepen

your self-awareness. Questions like "How do I respond when someone cuts in line?" or "Do I say 'yes' when I want to say 'no'?" can reveal areas where assertiveness might be lacking.

5. **Set an intention for change**

   Based on your self-assessment, choose one small change to focus on, like speaking up in a team meeting or setting a clear boundary with a friend. Start with manageable goals to build confidence.

6. **Be kind to yourself**

   Remember, self-assessment is a process of growth, not judgment. Treat each insight as a tool for progress, and celebrate small improvements along the way.

Taking time to reflect on your communication style and practicing with intention will help you make steady progress toward becoming more assertive. The better you understand yourself, the more empowered you'll be to communicate confidently and clearly.

Chapter 3

Starting Strong!

Laying the Groundwork for Assertive Confidence

"You teach people how to treat you by what you allow, what you stop, and what you reinforce." — Tony Gaskins

Here's a straightforward riddle:

I speak without shouting

I stand without pushing

I listen without interrupting,

I ask without demanding.

What am I?

The answer to the riddle is **"Assertiveness."** It is the ability to communicate your thoughts, feelings, and needs clearly and respectfully without being passive or aggressive. When you're assertive, you speak up for yourself without shouting, stand your ground without being pushy, and listen to others without cutting them off. It's a balance of self-respect and respect for others.

What to Expect: Here, you'll learn the essential traits that underlie assertive communication, including self-esteem, recognizing your rights, and harnessing positive body language. This chapter lays the groundwork for building assertiveness skills with integrity, helping you appreciate that assertiveness starts with self-respect and extends to respecting others.

As we move into this chapter, we'll explore how assertiveness is built on a strong sense of self-worth and a clear understanding of one's personal rights. Just like the qualities in the riddle, assertiveness is about finding that middle ground where one can express oneself confidently and respectfully in any situation.

By the end of this chapter, you'll better grasp what it takes to be assertive, and you'll be ready to apply these ideas in your everyday life.

Reflective Question: When you think about your self-worth, do you believe you deserve the same respect and consideration as others, or do you often place your needs and opinions second? Why do you think that is?

Building Self-Esteem and Confidence

When it comes to assertiveness, high self-esteem is not just a bonus—it's essential. Self-esteem allows you to recognize your values, believe that your needs and opinions are important, and confidently express them. Without a strong sense of self-worth, it's easy to fall into patterns of passivity or shy away from standing up for yourself.

Here are a couple of practical tips to help you start building the self-esteem that will support your journey to becoming more assertive:

- **Daily Affirmations**: Repeated actions become behavior; the same principle applies to the thoughts you reinforce in your mind. Regularly affirming positive statements can influence your beliefs and personality over time. This is the power of autosuggestion, which is used in cognitive behavior therapies.

  Begin each day by affirming your worth and capabilities. Look in the mirror and speak positive statements about yourself, such as "I am good," "I am capable," "My opinions are valuable," or "I deserve respect." Do not pretend; be sure to believe what you speak is true.

One autosuggestion script I found very effective with my clients comes from the Silva Mind Control Method. It goes like this: ***Evey day, in every way, I am getting better, better, and better!*** Consider using it as a mantra; print it out and stick it on your bedroom wall to see every day when you wake up and when you return to bed. Let it sink into your subconscious.

These affirmations might feel awkward at first, but over time, they can help rewire your mindset to focus on your strengths and potential.

- **Achievements Log**: Keep a journal where you record your daily achievements, no matter how small they may seem. Did you complete a task at work? Did you manage to get through a challenging conversation? Write it down. (A simple template is given in Appendix 3).

    This practice serves as a reminder of your abilities and accomplishments, helping you see your progress each day. It's a simple but powerful way to boost your confidence and reinforce your sense of self-worth.

Building self-esteem is a process, and it's okay if it takes time. The key is consistency—by regularly practicing these tips, you'll notice a shift in how you view yourself and your place in the world. As your self-esteem grows, so will your confidence in expressing your needs and standing up for yourself. And with that confidence, assertiveness becomes a natural extension of who you are.

Reflective Question: How might your communication change if you truly believed in your worth?

Behavioral Experiment: Putting Assertiveness to the Test

Building confidence in your assertiveness isn't just about shifting your mindset; it's also about taking small, practical steps to see how different responses work in real situations. One of the most effective ways to do this is through a **Behavioral Experiment**. In Cognitive Behavioral Therapy (CBT), a behavioral experiment is a way to test out new behaviors, assess their impact, and learn from the experience. It's about moving from theory to action, one small step at a time.

When it comes to assertiveness, trying out a new behavior can feel intimidating, especially if you've spent years in people-pleasing mode. A behavioral experiment allows you to try being assertive in a controlled way, helping you build confidence and see that the consequences are often far less intimidating than you might imagine.

Exercise: Designing Your Assertiveness Experiment

Follow these steps to set up and complete a behavioral experiment that helps you take small, manageable steps toward assertiveness.

1. **Choose a Small Assertive Action**: Identify a low-stakes situation where you'd like to be more

assertive. This might be something like expressing a minor preference (e.g., suggesting where to go for lunch with a friend) or setting a small boundary (e.g., letting a coworker know that you're not available after hours).

2. **Make a Prediction**: Write down what you expect will happen if you act assertively in this situation. Do you think the other person will react negatively, or will they be supportive? How do you think you'll feel afterward?

3. **Plan Your Approach**: Decide how you'll carry out the assertive action. For example, if you're setting a boundary, plan the words you'll use (e.g., "I'd love to help, but I'm already committed to another project right now"). Keep it simple and direct.

4. **Take Action**: Carry out your planned assertive behavior. Remember that this is a learning exercise, so try not to worry about getting it perfect. Focus on speaking clearly and calmly.

5. **Observe the Outcome**: After you complete the action, write down what actually happened. Did the other person respond as you predicted? How did you feel afterward? Rate your feelings from 1–10 to gauge the emotional impact of the experiment.

6. **Reflect on What You Learned**: Compare your prediction to the actual outcome. What did you learn from this experience? Did anything surprise you?

Consider whether you'd be willing to try a similar action again in the future.

Example Behavioral Experiment

Here's an example of how a behavioral experiment might look in practice:

- **Chosen Action**: Politely declining a friend's invitation when I need time to recharge.

- **Prediction**: I'll feel guilty, and my friend might feel hurt or think I'm being selfish.

- **Planned Approach**: I'll say, "Thanks so much for the invite! I've had a busy week and need some quiet time, but let's plan to meet up next week instead."

- **Outcome**: My friend understood right away and said she could relate to needing downtime. I felt relieved and empowered.

- **Reflection**: I learned that setting boundaries doesn't necessarily hurt others—it actually feels good to be honest about my needs. I'm willing to try this again in other situations.

By conducting behavioral experiments, you'll begin to gather real evidence that supports assertive communication. Each time you see that an assertive action didn't lead to a feared outcome—or that the benefits outweighed the challenges—you'll gain confidence to be more assertive in other areas of your life.

Try It!

Choose one small action this week to experiment with. Approach it as a curious observer, looking for what you can learn rather than aiming for perfection. The goal is not only to act assertively but to understand that assertiveness is a skill you can strengthen one step at a time.

As you conduct these experiments, you'll find that assertiveness becomes less intimidating and more natural. With each success, you're reinforcing your self-worth and building the confidence to stand tall in your interactions.

Understanding Your Rights and Responsibilities

A key part of being assertive is having a clear understanding of your own rights in any interaction, as well as the responsibilities that come with those rights. Assertiveness is about finding a balance between standing up for yourself and respecting others, and that balance hinges on knowing where your rights end and your responsibilities begin.

Your Rights

You have the right to express your thoughts, beliefs, and feelings. This is fundamental to assertiveness. You're entitled to share your opinions, to ask for what you need, and to voice your feelings without fear of being dismissed or invalidated. Your voice matters whether in personal relationships, work, or any other context, and you have every right to use it.

But with this right comes the responsibility to ensure that your expression doesn't harm or diminish others. This is where assertiveness differs from aggression.

Your Responsibilities

While you have the right to speak your mind, you also have the responsibility to do so in a way that is respectful and considerate of others. As stated in an earlier chapter, assertiveness is not about bulldozing over someone else's thoughts or feelings; it's about creating a space where both your needs and theirs can coexist. This means expressing yourself clearly and confidently but without infringing on the rights of others to do the same.

In practice, this might mean being mindful of your tone, choosing your words carefully, and listening as much as you speak. It's about being firm in your stance but also open to hearing and respecting the perspectives of those around you.

Understanding these rights and responsibilities is crucial because they form the foundation of healthy, balanced interactions. When you know your rights, you're empowered to stand up for yourself. When you embrace your responsibilities, you can strengthen your relationships and foster mutual respect.

As you work to become more assertive, keep these

principles in mind. They will guide you in difficult conversations, help you make decisions that honor both yourself and others, and ultimately, help you build more meaningful and respectful connections in every area of your life.

The Role of Body Language

Assertiveness isn't just conveyed through your chosen words—it's also about how you deliver those words. Your body language and tone of voice are powerful tools that can either reinforce or undermine the message you're trying to communicate. They are critical in how others perceive your confidence, intentions, and respect for the conversation.

Your body language—the way you hold yourself, your facial expressions, eye contact, gestures, and posture—speaks volumes and can even change how others perceive you. Understanding the different types of body language is essential for developing a clear, confident, respectful, and assertive communication style. Below, we'll explore three types of body language relevant to assertiveness: **Assertive**, **Passive**, and **Aggressive**.[1]

Assertive Body Language: Confident and Open

Assertive body language strikes a balance between

---

[1] Note: For a comprehensive insight into body language, see: Pease, Allan, and Barbara Pease. *The Definitive Book of Body Language: The Hidden Meaning Behind People's Gestures and Expressions*. Bantam, 2006.

confidence and approachability. When communicating assertively, you're conveying self-respect and respect for others, making it clear that your voice is valuable but not at the expense of others.

Key Characteristics

- **Posture**: Stand or sit up straight with your shoulders relaxed but not slouched. This shows confidence and readiness to engage without seeming overbearing.

- **Eye Contact**: Make regular eye contact, holding it for a few seconds at a time. It signals attentiveness and openness but avoids staring, which can feel confrontational.

- **Facial Expression**: Maintain a relaxed, pleasant facial expression. A gentle smile or neutral expression communicates calmness and receptiveness.

- **Gestures**: Use open and deliberate hand gestures. Avoid crossing your arms (a defensive gesture), and try to keep your hands visible. Gesturing occasionally with palms open can signal honesty and transparency.

- **Personal Space**: Stand at a comfortable distance, typically 2-3 feet, to respect others' personal space while remaining close enough to engage.

- **Eye contact**: Maintaining eye contact shows that you are attentive and confident in your communication. It signals that you're open to dialogue and fully present in the conversation. Not making eye contact, on the other hand, can give the impression of insecurity or disinterest.

- **Good posture**: When you stand or sit upright, with your back straight and shoulders slightly thrown backward, it means that you are confident. It speaks strength and self-confidence. It is an easy thing to adjust and can make a huge difference in how you are seen by others.

- **Open gestures**: Using your hands and arms can also help to convey assertiveness. Open gestures, such as keeping your hands visible and using them to emphasize points, suggest that you're approachable and sincere. Do not cross your arms as much as possible because they can look defensive and uninterested.

Passive Body Language: Closed and Hesitant

Passive body language often indicates discomfort or reluctance to express oneself. This style can unintentionally signal a lack of confidence, making it easy for others to overlook or interrupt the person communicating.

Key Characteristics

- **Posture**: Slumped shoulders, or leaning away from others, conveys a lack of self-assurance. Avoiding a straight, balanced posture may signal that the person feels vulnerable.

- **Eye Contact**: Limited or indirect eye contact—looking down or away frequently—can signal insecurity or reluctance to engage.

- **Facial Expression**: A tense or overly neutral expression, or biting one's lip, suggests discomfort or hesitation.

- **Gestures**: Minimal gestures, often with hands kept close to the body or hidden, can signal uncertainty. Fidgeting, like touching the face or wringing hands, can convey nervousness.

- **Personal Space**: Passive communicators might stand farther back than necessary, indicating reluctance to engage or discomfort in the conversation.

Aggressive Body Language: Dominant and Closed-Off

Aggressive body language often comes across as hostile or intimidating, creating a barrier to respectful and open communication. This style can cause others to feel defensive or uncomfortable, undermining the intention of assertive expression.

Key Characteristics

- **Posture**: Standing too close to others, puffing out the chest, or leaning forward aggressively can feel physically imposing.

- **Eye Contact**: Intense, prolonged eye contact (often staring) can feel like a challenge or threat, creating tension.

- **Facial Expression**: A furrowed brow, clenched jaw, or narrowed eyes may indicate anger or frustration.

- **Gestures**: Pointing or jabbing fingers, making abrupt hand movements, or crossing arms tightly over the chest signal dominance or impatience.

- **Personal Space**: Aggressive communicators often invade personal space, standing too close or leaning in forcefully.

Confident Tone

How you speak those words is very important. A confident voice will ensure that your message is heard how you intended it to be:

- **Clarity of speech**: It is key to assertiveness. Speaking clearly makes you sound thoughtful and deliberate. Speaking calmly, without rushing or raising your voice, shows control and composure, even in a possibly tense situation.

- **Keep your voice steady**: A steady voice indicates confidence and self-assurance. Ensure that your tone does not waver or trail off towards the end of sentences, as this portrays uncertainty. Using a steady voice says that you are confident in your message and stand by what you say.

Positive body language and a confident tone of voice create a powerful combination that enhances your assertiveness. They aid you in expressing not just what words come out of your mouth- but also how confident and respectful they sound. You will likely be heard, understood, and respected when your body language and tone align with your message. These non-verbal cues are essential in your communication toolkit, helping you express yourself in a confident and considerate way.

Type of Body Language	Eye Contact	Posture	Facial Expression	Gestures	Personal Space
Assertive	Holds natural, steady eye contact, without staring.	Upright, balanced posture; shoulders relaxed.	Relaxed, calm expression; gentle smile or neutral.	Open, visible hands with deliberate movements; palms open.	Maintains respectful distance (2-3 feet).
Passive	Minimal or indirect eye contact; often looks down or away.	Slouched or closed posture; leaning away.	Tense, neutral, or uneasy; biting lip or avoiding smile.	Limited gestures; hands close to the body, often fidgeting.	Stands farther away, indicating discomfort.
Aggressive	Intense, prolonged eye contact; may stare.	Dominating, leaning in or invading space; chest puffed.	Tense, furrowed brows, clenched jaw; narrowed eyes.	Pointing, jabbing fingers; crossed arms; quick, sharp movements.	Stands very close, potentially invading personal space.

Reflective Question: Think of a situation where your body language or tone might have undermined your words. How could you adjust these in future interactions?

Emily's Transformation

Emily had always been seen as the quiet one in the room—timid, reserved, and often unsure of herself. In team meetings, she typically slouched in her chair, spoke softly, and rarely pushed her ideas forward, even when she knew she had something valuable to contribute. She would often leave these meetings feeling overlooked and frustrated, her self-esteem quietly eroding with each passing day.

But Emily knew she wanted more than just to blend into the background. She wanted to be heard, respected, and seen as a valuable contributor to her team. Determined to change, she focused on the two things she could control: her posture and voice.

At the next team meeting, Emily consciously decided to do things differently. Instead of slouching, she sat up straight, with her shoulders back and head held high. She didn't mumble or trail off when it came time for her to speak. She took a deep breath, projected her voice clearly, and confidently shared her ideas with the group.

The response was immediate. Her colleagues looked directly at her, agreeing and engaging with her ideas. There was a noticeable shift in the room; Emily wasn't just heard—she was listened to. The respect and attention she received were palpable, and it was clear that her presence was finally being acknowledged in the way she had always wanted.

This experience was a turning point for Emily. The positive reaction from her team reinforced her self-esteem and validated her new approach. She realized that by adjusting her posture and speaking confidently, she could completely transform how others perceived and responded to her.

From that day on, Emily made a commitment to maintain this new level of assertiveness. Her transformation didn't just stop at team meetings—it spilled over into every aspect of her work life. She became more proactive, more engaged, and more confident in all of her interactions. The impact on her career was significant, but the real change was within her. Emily's newfound assertiveness wasn't just about getting others to listen; it was about finally recognizing her worth and stepping into her power.

Emily's story is a powerful reminder that assertiveness isn't always about making grand gestures or radical changes. Sometimes, small, deliberate adjustments—like standing tall and speaking up—can have the most profound impact. And as Emily discovered, these changes don't just alter how others see you—they transform how you see yourself.

Balancing Confidence with Approachability

Here's a heads-up! While developing assertiveness, you might wonder if being confident will come across as "too strong" or intimidating. It's normal to have this concern, but it doesn't mean it's true. Assertiveness involves clearly expressing your needs and boundaries, but it doesn't have to be inflexible, dominating, arrogant, or overpowering. In fact, balancing confidence with approachability can make your assertive communication feel more natural and effective.

When you're confident, you stand by your needs with self-respect, yet being approachable means leaving room for the other person's thoughts and feelings. This balance can make you more relatable and even encourage others to respond openly.

To maintain this balance, please follow these steps:

- **Use warm body language**: Maintain a confident posture with an open, relaxed facial expression. Eye contact is important, but soften it by allowing natural breaks—no need to "lock-in." A slight smile can signal that while you're firm, you're also friendly.

- **Listen actively**: Assertiveness includes being a good listener. Show genuine interest in the other person's viewpoint by nodding occasionally and making supportive sounds ("I see," "Okay," etc.). This conveys that you're still open to understanding their perspective while standing your ground.

- **Express empathy**: Assertiveness doesn't mean avoiding all emotions. Letting the other person know you understand their feelings can build rapport. For instance, you might say, "I understand this is important to you," before stating your needs. This reassures them that you respect their views.

When you balance confidence with approachability, assertiveness feels more conversational and collaborative. It's about standing tall while staying open and letting others see that assertiveness and kindness can go hand in hand.

Recap

Building the foundations of assertiveness is about much more than just learning to speak up—it's about developing a strong and resilient sense of self, understanding your rights in any interaction, and mastering the ability to convey your thoughts and needs clearly and confidently. These core elements are the bedrock upon which true assertiveness is built, and they are essential for navigating personal and professional relationships with respect and integrity.

In this chapter, we've explored the vital components that make assertiveness possible. You've learned the importance of cultivating high self-esteem, which gives you the confidence to value your voice and stand up for what you believe in. We've also discussed the necessity of recognizing your rights and responsibilities in communication, ensuring that you express yourself in a way that is both assertive and respectful of others.

Moreover, we discussed the critical role that body language and tone play in how your messages are received. Assertiveness isn't just about what you say but how you say it. How you carry yourself and your confidence in your voice can be as impactful as your chosen words.

The tools and insights provided in this chapter are designed to help you start building these foundational skills. Integrating these principles into your daily interactions will make you more confident, respected, and effective in your communication.

This chapter has set the stage for the more advanced techniques in assertiveness communication that we'll explore in the upcoming chapters. With a strong foundation, you're now ready to dive deeper into the strategies that will help you apply assertiveness in various real-life situations. Remember, assertiveness is a journey that requires practice, patience, and persistence. But with these foundational skills, you're well on your way to mastering the art of assertive communication.

Reflective Question: What step can you take this week to strengthen your foundational assertiveness skills?

In Practice: Key Steps for Building Assertiveness Foundations

1. **Build Self-Esteem through positive self-talk**

    Practice daily affirmations or positive self-talk to

reinforce your self-worth. Statements like "I deserve respect" or "My opinions are valuable" can help shift your mindset over time.

2. **Understand your rights and responsibilities**

   Recognize that you have the right to express your thoughts, needs, and boundaries respectfully. At the same time, remember to honor others' rights by listening and responding with empathy.

3. **Practice assertive body language**

   Focus on non-verbal cues: stand or sit up straight, maintain comfortable eye contact, and use open gestures. These small changes can make a big difference in conveying confidence and respect.

4. **Use a calm, steady tone**

   When speaking, aim for a clear, steady tone of voice. This shows confidence and helps you express yourself without coming across as passive or aggressive.

5. **Check in with your self-worth regularly**

   Reflect on how you view your own worth. If you often place others' needs above your own, remind yourself that your needs are equally important. Practicing assertiveness begins with believing in your value.

6. **Start small with assertive actions**

   Choose one area where you can practice

assertiveness, like speaking clearly in a meeting or setting a personal boundary with a friend. These small, intentional actions help you strengthen your assertive foundation.

By building a foundation of self-respect, assertive body language, and mindful tone, you're setting yourself up for success in more challenging interactions. Remember, these skills take practice—begin with small steps and watch your confidence grow.

Chapter 4

Speak Your Truth!

Techniques for Clear, Confident Communication

"Raise your words, not your voice. It is rain that grows flowers, not thunder." — Rumi

Effective communication is not just about speaking your mind; it's about doing so clearly, directly, and respectfully. Though mentioned earlier, let me reiterate here. *The ability to express your thoughts, feelings, and needs confidently while also considering the perspectives of others is what truly sets assertive communication apart.* If it lacks respect, it's far from assertiveness but can be interpreted as arrogance, rudeness, or stubbornness.

What to Expect: This chapter introduces practical techniques like "I" statements, active listening, and refusal skills. These tools are designed to help you communicate confidently and clearly, minimizing misunderstandings. By mastering these techniques, you'll be better equipped to express your needs effectively while maintaining positive relationships.

In this chapter, we'll explore practical techniques that will help you refine your communication skills and ensure that your messages are understood as you intend. These techniques are designed to empower you to articulate your ideas without hesitation and to address challenges in a way that fosters mutual respect and understanding.

Objectives?

- You may be engaging in a difficult conversation
- You may be trying to set boundaries
- You want to express your needs more clearly

The strategies outlined in this chapter will give you the tools to communicate more effectively. By mastering these techniques, you'll improve your interactions and minimize the risk of misunderstandings that can lead to conflict or frustration.

Reflective Question: How do you typically express your needs or disagree with someone? Do you find it effective?

"I" Statements and Active Listening

A cornerstone of assertive communication is the ability to express your thoughts and feelings in a way that is both honest and non-confrontational. One of the most effective ways to do this is by using "I" statements. Unlike "you" statements, which can often come across as accusatory or critical, "I" statements allow you to own your feelings and communicate them without placing blame on others. This approach fosters a more open and constructive dialogue, reducing the likelihood of defensiveness and conflict.

Using "I" Statements[2]

"I" statements help you express your feelings and needs without making the other person feel accountable or responsible. This technique shifts the focus from what the other person did wrong to how their actions affected you, which encourages a more empathetic response.

Example of an "I" Statement: Instead of saying, "You never listen to me," which may make the other person feel defensive, try saying, "I feel unheard when you interrupt me during our conversations." This statement clearly communicates your feelings while also inviting the other person to consider their behavior without feeling blamed.

By framing your concerns this way, you create a space for constructive conversation and collaboration, rather than conflict.

A Quick Look at the ABC Model in Action

To understand the ABC Model, let's start with a quick example to see how it works in action. I will elaborate it after. Picture yourself in a meeting. You're sharing an idea, and suddenly, a colleague interrupts you—more than once. This situation is the **Activating Event** (A), a trigger, the

---

[2] *For specific examples of "I" statements you can use in various situations, refer to Appendix 6: Examples of "I" Statements for Different Scenarios. These can help you get started with clear, respectful expressions of your thoughts, needs, and feelings.*

moment that starts your reaction.

You might find yourself thinking, "If I speak up, they'll think I'm overreacting," or "I should just stay quiet to keep the peace." These thoughts form your **Belief** (B). And they lead you to a predictable **Consequence** (C): feeling frustrated and let down because you stayed silent when you actually wanted to speak up.

The ABC Model is designed to help identify these beliefs and consider new, more helpful ways of responding. By recognizing the belief ("They'll think I'm overreacting"), you can look at it differently, maybe by reminding yourself, "It's okay to calmly ask for a chance to finish—I deserve to be heard." With this shift, you might feel more comfortable saying, "I'd like to finish my thought," rather than staying silent and feeling resentful.

Now, let's see how it looks in real situations.

Understanding and Reframing Responses

Our beliefs shape our responses in every interaction. Sometimes, these beliefs can unintentionally hold us back from assertive communication. The **ABC Model**—a foundational tool in Cognitive Behavioral Therapy (CBT)—helps break down reactions to challenging situations and identify beliefs that may be influencing your responses.

By using this model, you'll learn to identify the beliefs that lead to unassertive behavior, such as staying silent, backing down, or agreeing to things you'd rather not.

Once you recognize these beliefs, you can start challenging them and adopt more balanced perspectives.

Understanding the ABC Model

The ABC Model breaks down your reaction into three parts:

1. **Activating Event (A)**: This is the situation that triggers your reaction. For example, someone interrupts you in a meeting, or a friend asks you to do something you're not comfortable with.

2. **Belief (B)**: This is the automatic thought or assumption you have about the situation. For instance, you might think, "If I speak up, they'll think I'm rude," or "I should go along with it to avoid disappointing them."

3. **Consequence (C)**: This is how the belief makes you feel and behave. If your belief is, "They'll think I'm rude if I assert myself," the consequence might be that you stay quiet or agree to something you don't want to do.

By understanding the ABCs of your responses, you can start to notice patterns and reframe unhelpful beliefs that prevent assertiveness.

Exercise: Reframing Your Beliefs with the ABC Model

Let's put the ABC Model into action. Use the following steps to work through a recent interaction where you felt challenged to communicate assertively.

1. **Identify the activating event**: Think of a specific situation where you struggled to assert yourself. Write down what happened, who was involved, and any details that come to mind.

2. **Identify your belief**: Ask yourself, "What thought went through my mind at that moment?" Be as specific as possible. Were you worried about upsetting someone? Did you fear judgment or conflict?

3. **Describe the consequence**: What emotion did the belief cause, and how did you respond? Did you feel anxious or guilty? Did you avoid speaking up or go along with something that didn't feel right?

4. **Challenge and reframe the belief**: Now, consider whether the belief was accurate or helpful. Ask yourself, "Is there another way to look at this situation?" or "What might be a more balanced belief that would help me act assertively?"

5. **Plan a new response**: Based on the new, balanced belief, write down how you might handle a similar situation in the future. Imagine using an "I" statement or calmly expressing your preference.

Example of the ABC Model in Action

Let's look at an example of the ABC Model in practice to illustrate how reframing beliefs can lead to more assertive responses:

- **Activating Event (A)**: A coworker interrupts you several times during a team meeting.

- **Belief (B)**: "If I say something, they'll think I'm difficult to work with."

- **Consequence (C)**: You stay quiet, feeling frustrated and undervalued.

Challenge and reframe: Is this belief accurate? Could it be that your coworker didn't realize they were interrupting? A more balanced belief might be, "It's reasonable to ask for a chance to speak. My input is valuable, and others will appreciate my perspective."

New response: Next time, use an "I" statement to express your need to be heard. For example, say, "I'd like to finish my thought before we move on. I think it could add value to the discussion."

Try It!

Reflect on a recent situation where you felt hesitant to speak up or set a boundary. Work through the ABCs to uncover the belief that shaped your response and consider how you might reframe it. Practicing this exercise will help you become aware of automatic beliefs and develop new, assertive responses.

The ABC Model is a powerful tool because it shows you that thoughts, not just situations, influence how you respond. By adjusting your beliefs, you can replace reactive, unhelpful responses with thoughtful, assertive ones—helping you communicate confidently and authentically.

You are encouraged to practice this model weekly, noting any changes in your assertive communication. Over time, the ABC Model can transform how you perceive interactions, making assertiveness a natural, empowering part of your life.

The Importance of Active Listening

While expressing your thoughts assertively is crucial, equally important is your ability to listen actively. Active listening is more than just hearing the words being spoken—it involves fully engaging with the speaker, understanding their message, and responding thoughtfully. When you listen actively, you show the other person that their thoughts and feelings are valued, which is key to building mutual respect and understanding.

Here are some tips to enhance your active listening skills:

- **Nod and make eye contact**: Simple gestures like nodding and maintaining eye contact demonstrate that you are fully present and engaged in the conversation. This non-verbal feedback reassures the speaker that you are paying attention and that you care about what they are saying.

- **Paraphrase what the speaker has said**: After the speaker has finished, paraphrase or summarize their key points to confirm your understanding. For example, you might say, "So, what I'm hearing is that you feel frustrated when deadlines aren't clearly communicated. Is that correct?" This not only shows that you've been listening carefully but also gives the speaker a chance to clarify if needed.

By combining the use of "I" statements with active listening, you can create more balanced and effective communication. This approach ensures that your needs are expressed clearly while also showing respect and consideration for the other person's perspective. When both parties feel heard and understood, the conversation is more likely to lead to positive outcomes and stronger relationships.

Reflective Question: Think of a recent conflict. How could "I" statements and active listening have changed the outcome?

Refusal Techniques

Mastering the Art of Saying No[3]

Saying no is one of the most essential skills in assertive communication, yet it's something many people struggle with. The fear of disappointing others or being perceived as uncooperative often leads to overcommitting or agreeing to things we don't really want to do. However, learning to say no confidently and without guilt is crucial for maintaining your boundaries and protecting your time and

---

[3] For additional guidance on phrasing assertive responses, refer to Appendix 4: Practical Conversation Starters for Assertive Communication. These examples can help you frame your responses in a variety of common situations, making it easier to communicate clearly and confidently.

energy.

Refusing a request doesn't have to be uncomfortable or confrontational. When done with respect and clarity, a refusal can actually strengthen your relationships by setting clear expectations and showing that you value your own needs as well as those of others.

Here are some steps to help you politely and assertively say no:

Steps to Politely Refuse[4]

- **Be direct and clear**: The first step in saying no is to be straightforward. Use clear, unambiguous language to communicate your refusal. There's no need to be overly apologetic or to soften your stance with vague language. For example, instead of saying, "I'm not sure if I can," say, "I don't have the capacity to take on that task right now." Being direct ensures that your message is understood and leaves little room for misinterpretation.

- **Offer an explanation if appropriate**: Depending on the situation, it can be helpful to provide a brief explanation for your refusal. This doesn't mean you have to justify your decision or provide a lengthy rationale, but a simple explanation can help the other person understand your perspective. For example, you might

---

[4] For more examples on saying "no" politely and assertively in various situations, refer to Appendix 5: Refusal Phrases for Assertive Communication. These phrases provide quick ways to set boundaries while keeping interactions respectful and considerate.

say, "I'm currently focusing on another project that requires my full attention." This kind of transparency shows that your refusal is not personal but rather based on your current commitments.

- **Suggest an alternative**: If possible, consider offering an alternative solution. This can soften the impact of your refusal and demonstrate your willingness to help in a different way. For example, you could say, "I can't take on this task, but I can help you find someone who might be able to assist," or "I'm unable to attend the meeting, but I can review the notes afterward." Providing an alternative shows that you're still engaged and supportive, even if you can't fulfill the original request.

Mastering the art of saying no is about balancing your own needs with the desire to maintain positive relationships. When you refuse a request with clarity and respect, you're not only setting healthy boundaries for yourself but also fostering honest and transparent communication with others. Remember, it's okay to prioritize your own well-being, and learning to say no is a decisive step toward achieving that balance.

How to Express Feelings and Needs Clearly

A key aspect of assertive communication is the ability to express your feelings and needs with clarity and confidence. Whether you're advocating for yourself in a work setting, addressing an issue in a personal relationship, or simply asking for something you need, being clear and direct is essential to ensure your message is understood and respected.

However, many of us struggle with expressing our needs clearly, often out of fear of being perceived as demanding or confrontational. Yet, when you communicate your feelings and needs effectively, you're not only standing up for yourself but also fostering healthier, more transparent relationships.

Here are some tips to help you express your feelings and needs more clearly:

Tips for Clear Expression

- **Be specific and straightforward**: When communicating your needs or feelings, it's crucial to be as specific as possible. Vague statements can lead to misunderstandings or leave the other person unsure of what you're really asking for. For example, instead of saying, "I need more help around the house," try saying, "I would appreciate it if you could take care of the dishes after dinner each night." The more precise you are, the easier it is for others to understand and respond to your needs.

- **Avoid qualifiers that weaken your message**: Words like "maybe," "probably," or "I guess" can undermine the strength of your message, making you sound uncertain or hesitant. These qualifiers dilute the clarity and impact of your communication. Instead, use confident language that reflects your true intentions. For instance, rather than saying, "I might need some time to myself," say, "I need some time to myself this evening." Clear and assertive language leaves no room for doubt.

- **Practice in low-stress situations**: If you find it challenging to express your feelings and needs clearly, start by practicing in situations where the stakes are lower. This could be with a close friend or family member or even in everyday scenarios like ordering food at a restaurant or asking for assistance in a store. As you build confidence in these low-pressure settings, you'll find it easier to communicate assertively in more significant, high-stress situations.

Clear expression is a skill that, like any other, improves with practice. The more you focus on being specific, eliminating unnecessary qualifiers, and gradually building your confidence, the more natural and effective your communication will become. By expressing your feelings and needs clearly, you're not only ensuring that your voice is heard but also creating the foundation for more honest, respectful, and fulfilling interactions.

Reflective Question: Are there situations where you struggle to express your needs? Why do you think that is?

John's Promotion Request

Meet John, one of the people I collaborated with on a project. I found something common between us in terms of a people-pleasing attitude. He never asked for anything, as he always expected his manager to see John's dedication and hard work without John giving updates regarding how he had been working hard.

Over the years, he consistently met and exceeded his performance goals, taking on additional responsibilities and making significant contributions to his team. He believed in doing rather than presenting himself and talking for himself at team meetings. He worked hard, but his files often didn't reflect his work as he never thought about the importance of recording his activities or believed that doing was far more important than recording.

However, despite his efforts, he had never formally requested a promotion, often assuming that his work would speak for itself. As time passed, John realized that he needed to take a more proactive approach to advancing in his career. He understood that nobody would notice his contributions and commitments unless he spoke for himself. In other words, nobody would see his contributions if he didn't speak for himself. Self-promotion is very important, as he realized.

Also, it was painful for John to observe some of his colleagues, whom he knew were not as hardworking as him, present themselves at team meetings, confidently presenting their cases and receiving high appreciation from the manager and other team members.

Determined to secure the promotion he felt he deserved, John turned to the assertive communication techniques he had been learning. He knew that simply mentioning his achievements in passing wouldn't be enough—he needed to clearly and confidently articulate his value to the company and make his case for why he was ready for the next step in his career.

As his annual performance review approached, John carefully prepared. He focused on crafting strong "I" statements that would highlight his accomplishments without sounding boastful. He wanted to ensure that his contributions were clearly communicated and that his request for a promotion was both respectful and direct.

When the day of the review arrived, John was ready. Sitting down with his boss, he began by summarizing his key achievements from the past year. "I have successfully completed all my project goals this year," he stated confidently, "and I also took the initiative to develop and lead a new training program that has significantly improved team performance." John made sure to emphasize the impact of his work on the company's success.

Then, without hesitation, he moved on to his request. "I believe that these achievements demonstrate my readiness for increased responsibilities, and I would like to discuss the possibility of a promotion to the next level in my career." John's tone was clear and composed, leaving no doubt about his intentions.

His boss listened intently, impressed not only by John's accomplishments but also by the clarity and confidence with which he presented them. The preparation and thoughtfulness John had put into his request were evident, and his boss appreciated the direct yet respectful way he approached the conversation.

Thanks to his assertive communication, John's request was well-received. His manager acknowledged his hard work and contributions, agreeing that a promotion was indeed warranted.

John's experience is a powerful example of how assertive communication can significantly improve one's achievement of career goals. By preparing thoroughly, using clear "I" statements, and expressing his desires confidently,

John was able to successfully advocate for himself and take the next step in his professional journey.

What lessons can we learn from John's story?

- Do not assume that others will understand you from your performance.

- Doing and reporting are equally important. If you don't record and/or report, people will not know about your performance.

- If you don't speak for yourself, nobody will speak for you.

- Don't assume that people will understand your expectations without you raising them.

- Use "I" statements, be clear about what you want to say, and speak confidently.

Conclusion

In this chapter, you've gained a set of powerful tools designed to enhance your ability to communicate assertively. From learning the importance of "I" statements to mastering the art of active listening, you now have the fundamental techniques needed to express your thoughts, feelings, and needs in a way that is both clear and respectful.

We also explored the critical skill of saying no with confidence through effective refusal techniques. Understanding how to set boundaries without guilt is key to maintaining your well-being while respecting the needs of others. Additionally, you've learned how to articulate your desires and emotions directly without diminishing your message or undermining your intentions.

These techniques are more than just communication strategies—they are the building blocks of assertive interactions that can positively impact every area of your life. Whether in the workplace, at home, or in social settings, these skills will empower you to express yourself with confidence and clarity, ensuring that your voice is heard and your boundaries are respected.

As you continue to practice and refine these techniques, you'll find that assertive communication becomes a natural and integral part of how you interact with the world. The ability to communicate effectively is a lifelong skill that not only improves your relationships but also strengthens your sense of self and your overall well-being.

With these tools in hand, you're well on your way to becoming a more assertive, confident, and empowered communicator. In the chapters ahead, we'll build on these foundational skills, exploring more advanced strategies for navigating complex interactions and fostering positive, productive relationships.

Reflective Question: Which communication technique will you commit to practicing this week? How will you implement it?

In Practice: Key Steps for Using Assertive Communication Techniques

1. **Use "I" statements to express your feelings**

   Practice framing your thoughts with "I" statements, like "I feel…" or "I need…" This shifts the focus to your experience without sounding accusatory, helping keep conversations open and constructive.

2. **Listen actively**

   Show you're engaged by making eye contact, nodding, and paraphrasing what the other person says. Active listening builds mutual respect and helps prevent misunderstandings.

3. **Say "No" with confidence**

   Politely decline requests by keeping your language clear and direct. Phrases like "I won't be able to help with that right now" are effective ways to set boundaries without feeling guilty.

4. **Express needs clearly and directly**

   When asking for support or explaining a need, be specific and avoid softening your language with qualifiers like "maybe" or "I guess." Clear statements are key, such as "I need time to focus on this project."

5. **Prepare for challenging conversations**

   If you anticipate a difficult discussion, rehearse what

you'd like to say. Practicing helps you feel more confident and reduces anxiety about potential conflict.

6. **Reflect after each interaction**

   After using an assertive communication technique, take a moment to reflect on the outcome. What worked well? What would you do differently next time? This self-reflection helps you refine your skills over time.

Remember, assertive communication is a skill that grows with practice—use these steps to build comfort and confidence in expressing your needs.

Chapter 5

When Sparks Fly

Standing Tall in Tough Conversations

"The ultimate measure of a man is not where he stands in moments of comfort and convenience, but where he stands at times of challenge and controversy." Martin Luther King Jr.

What to Expect: Conflict is normal and sometimes becomes inevitable, but this chapter equips you with the tools to handle it assertively and constructively. You'll learn techniques for managing confrontation calmly, seeking compromise, and staying composed under pressure. These skills will help you approach disagreements with confidence, turning conflicts into opportunities for growth.

From Silence to Self-Respect

When I first started my career, I held the belief that confronting someone or voicing disagreement would only lead to hurt feelings and conflict. I genuinely thought that staying silent was a way of preserving harmony, even at the cost of my own discomfort. The idea of speaking up for myself, offering critical feedback, or pointing out errors seemed risky—it felt like a surefire way to come off as rude or arrogant. So, I kept my thoughts to myself, even when I knew there were things that needed to change or improve.

Deep down, there was also a misguided sense of self-sacrifice that kept me quiet. I often thought, "If it makes them feel better to push me around or ignore my input, then so be it." I convinced myself that absorbing the discomfort was somehow noble, a silent act of keeping the peace. But over time, this approach chipped away at my confidence. It left me feeling invisible, unheard, and, at times, deeply frustrated.

Eventually, I had to face a hard truth: by choosing silence, I wasn't being kind to myself. I wasn't protecting my well-being or standing up for what I knew to be right. Instead, I was reinforcing a cycle of self-neglect that benefited no one—not me, not my colleagues, and certainly not the quality of our work together. Realizing this was the first step toward change, toward understanding that assertiveness, when done with respect, is a form of kindness—both to myself and to those around me.

It took me some time to learn that confronting others is not as bad as I thought. Moreover, it would help the other person finetune their approach or behavior. I only needed to be mindful of my approach while confronting them. I remember my professor speaking of *carefrontation*—confronting with care—as a powerful method rather than *correcting* others, which might put them on the defensive.

Decatastrophizing: Reducing Fear in Confrontation

For many, the fear of conflict or confrontation is rooted in worst-case scenarios—often imagining that speaking up could lead to anger, resentment, or even the loss of a relationship. This fear can be overwhelming, making assertive communication feel too risky. However, many of these scenarios are catastrophes our minds invent, based on fear rather than reality. *Decatastrophizing* is a technique from Cognitive Behavioral Therapy (CBT) that helps us look at these fears objectively, reducing their intensity and empowering us to act with confidence.

Conflict is an inevitable part of any relationship, be it personal or professional. Whether it arises from differing opinions, unmet expectations, or simply the pressures of daily life, conflict is something we all encounter. However, the way we handle these conflicts can make all the difference in maintaining healthy and respectful relationships.

With *decatastrophizing*, you examine the "worst-case" outcomes you're imagining, assessing whether they're realistic and exploring alternative, more balanced outcomes. This process helps you approach challenging the conflicting situations calmly, seeing them as opportunities for growth rather than potential disasters.

Exercise: Decatastrophizing Your Fears

Follow these steps to work through your fear of confrontation or assertiveness. Try using this exercise anytime you find yourself feeling overwhelmed by a situation where you'd like to assert yourself but feel hesitant.

1. **Identify the situation**: Think of a situation where you fear a negative outcome if you were to assert

yourself. For example, it could be a disagreement with a colleague or expressing your needs in a relationship.

2. **Write down your worst-case scenario**: What is the worst thing you believe could happen if you assert yourself? Be as detailed as possible. Do you imagine the other person getting angry, rejecting you, or the relationship being damaged?

3. **Assess the likelihood**: Now, take a step back and assess how realistic this outcome truly is. Ask yourself, "Has anything like this happened before? If so, did it play out as badly as I imagined?" Rate the likelihood of this worst-case scenario on a scale of 1–10.

4. **Consider the best-case scenario**: Imagine the best possible outcome if you were to act assertively. Could the other person respect your needs, agree to a compromise, or see your viewpoint? Write down this best-case scenario and rate its likelihood on a scale of 1–10.

5. **Explore the most likely scenario**: Now, identify what you think is the most likely outcome based on past experiences. For example, maybe they'll listen but may need time to process, or they might ask questions to understand better. Write down this balanced outcome, rating its likelihood on a scale of 1–10.

6. **Make a plan based on reality**: With a clearer perspective on what's most likely to happen, plan how you'll respond. If the worst case is unlikely, you can focus on expressing yourself confidently, knowing that the outcome is likely to be more positive than you initially thought.

Example of Decatastrophizing in Practice

Here's how this exercise might look in a real-life scenario:

- **Situation**: You want to ask a close friend to stop interrupting you during conversations.

- **Worst-case scenario**: "If I bring this up, they'll feel hurt, become defensive, and might even stop talking to me." (Likelihood: 3/10)

- **Best-case scenario**: "They'll understand and apologize, making an effort to listen more carefully." (Likelihood: 6/10)

- **Most likely scenario**: "They might be a bit surprised or embarrassed but will likely appreciate my honesty and make an effort to change." (Likelihood: 8/10)

Plan Based on Reality: Knowing that the worst-case scenario is unlikely, you decide to speak calmly and directly, using an "I" statement to express your needs. For example, "I feel unheard when I'm interrupted and would appreciate it if you could let me finish my thoughts before responding." By focusing on the most likely outcome, you feel less anxious about expressing yourself.

Try It!

Choose a situation you're currently facing where fear is holding you back from being assertive. Walk through the steps of this exercise, from identifying the worst-case scenario to creating a balanced plan based on the most likely outcome.

By practicing *decatastrophizing*, you'll start to see confrontations as opportunities to strengthen your communication rather than as situations to avoid. This tool will help you recognize that even if conflicts arise, you can approach them with a level head and find a solution that respects both your needs and those of others.

Over time, this skill will help you develop the confidence to confront challenging situations without letting fear dictate your actions, empowering you to stand tall in your interactions.

Aggression, Passivity, Arguing, Asserting

When faced with a dispute, it's easy to fall into the extremes of aggression or passivity, which is far from the *carefrontation* approach that we discussed. Aggression would never lead to a constructive resolution. It can escalate tensions and damage relationships, while passivity often results in unresolved issues and lingering resentment. The key lies in finding a middle ground—handling conflicts assertively.

Remember, giving direct correction will imply that something is not right with the other person. Nobody wants to feel that way, so they might try to defend themselves rather than reflect on their behavior or attitude. On the other hand, being assertive involves understanding and respecting, which would help the other person see your point.

Arguments come with emotions. They touch the ego. Their primary goal is to win a point. We often forget the hard reality that, through argument, we may win a point, but we will surely lose the person! So, it is not the way to go for sure.

Assertive conflict resolution is about standing up for your own needs and perspectives while also valuing and considering the needs and viewpoints of others. It's about navigating disagreements without compromising your integrity or the dignity of those involved.

We'll explore techniques that will help you stay calm and composed during conflicts, communicate your concerns clearly and respectfully, and work towards solutions that satisfy both parties. By the end of this chapter, you'll have the tools to approach conflicts with confidence, ensuring that both you and the other person feel heard, understood, and respected.

Reflective Question: Recall a recent conflict. Did the outcome feel fair to all involved? Why or why not?

Strategies for Negotiation and Compromise

Effective conflict resolution often hinges on the ability to negotiate and find a compromise that respects the needs and interests of all parties involved. For example, there may be conflicts regarding your manager's expectation of better output from you despite your struggle with a huge caseload and limited resources. Suppose you are not clarifying or asserting your position with your manager and negotiating an improved work environment and resources. In that case, your manager may get a different perspective that you are underperforming. This will create further conflict in terms of both parties' interests.

Negotiation isn't about winning or losing; it's about working together to reach a solution that everyone can agree on. When handled assertively, negotiation becomes a powerful tool for resolving conflicts in a way that strengthens relationships and fosters mutual respect.

Here are some key steps to guide you through the process of effective negotiation and compromise:

Steps for Effective Negotiation

- **Prepare: Understand your needs and the needs of the other party**

  The first step in any successful negotiation is preparation. Before you enter into a discussion, take the time to clearly identify your own needs, priorities, and non-negotiables. Equally important is to try to understand the needs and concerns of the other party. What are their priorities? What might they be willing to compromise on? By preparing thoroughly, you'll enter the negotiation with a clear sense of what you want to achieve and a better understanding of the other person's perspective.

- **Communicate: Use clear, assertive language to express your position**

  When it comes to negotiation, how you communicate is just as important as what you communicate. Use clear, assertive language to express your needs, desires, and concerns. Be specific about what you're asking for and why it matters to you. For example, instead of saying, "I'd like more flexibility," you might say, "I need a more flexible schedule to balance my work and personal responsibilities." By being direct and transparent, you make it easier for the other party to understand your position and engage in a constructive dialogue.

- **Listen: Pay attention to the other party's concerns and suggestions**

    Effective negotiation is a two-way street. While it's important to express your own needs, it's equally crucial to listen actively to what the other party has to say. Show that you're open to their perspective by asking questions, summarizing their points, and acknowledging their concerns. This not only demonstrates respect but also helps to build trust and rapport, making it more likely that both parties will be willing to work towards a compromise.

- **Propose Compromises: Offer solutions that address both parties' needs**

    Negotiation is often about finding a middle ground. Once you've clearly communicated your position and listened to the other party's concerns, it's time to propose compromises that can satisfy both sides. Think creatively about potential solutions and be willing to make concessions where possible. For instance, if you're negotiating a work schedule, you might suggest a trial period for the new arrangement, with a review after a few months. By proposing flexible and thoughtful compromises, you show that you're committed to finding a resolution that works for everyone.

During my work in the mental health team, I remember preparing a list of cases I was dealing with and several projects I was involved in. Attending my supervision with my manager became much easier when I had printed copies of this list for my manager and myself. The document clarified the workload, available resources, limitations, etc., and suggested solutions. The manager found it very helpful to agree on some solutions. The whole negotiation process would have become difficult without such clarity. During this process, I was asserting my needs by clarifying my situation while respecting my manager's position as my supervisor.

Negotiation and compromise are not about sacrificing your needs or overpowering the other party; they are about collaboration and mutual respect. When you approach negotiation with an assertive mindset, you pave the way for fair and balanced outcomes that leave all parties feeling valued and understood. By following these steps, you'll be better equipped to navigate conflicts with confidence and find solutions that strengthen your relationships and achieve positive results.

Look at that mirror; don't break it!

Criticism is something we all encounter, whether in our personal lives or professional settings. While receiving criticism can be uncomfortable, how you handle it plays a significant role in shaping the outcome of the interaction. When approached with an assertive mindset, criticism—no matter how challenging—can be transformed from a potentially negative experience into an opportunity for personal and professional growth.

Remember, if someone doesn't point out our mistakes, we will have no idea how to improve. So, it is better to approach every criticism as if you are looking at yourself in the mirror, seeing your own image, actions, and personality. Even if the criticism comes with some form of blame, it will help you to see whether you need some fine-tuning. Instead, if you decide to attack the criticizer, you are breaking the mirror. By doing that, you are losing an opportunity to see your image. Once you have a closer look and do not see something wrong with you, it will give you an excellent opportunity to clarify your position based on the evidence that you saw in the mirror reflection. This is asserting!

Tips for Dealing with Criticism

- **Listen Fully: Recognize the value of feedback**

    The first step in handling criticism assertively is to listen carefully to what's being said. Even when criticism feels harsh or unfair, it's important to stay open to the possibility that there may be valuable feedback within the message. This is how you look in the mirror. By fully listening, you show respect for the other person's perspective and give yourself a chance to identify areas where you might genuinely benefit from making that subtle adjustment. Remember, criticism—when constructive—can be a catalyst for growth.

Side note: I hate using the word 'change,' as it could imply that something is not right. I prefer 'Finetuning' instead.

- **Respond Calmly: Use "I" statements to maintain composure**

    When faced with criticism, it's natural to feel defensive, but reacting defensively can escalate the situation and hinder productive dialogue. Instead, respond calmly and use "I" statements to express your thoughts. For example, instead of saying, "You're wrong about my performance," try saying, "I feel that my recent contributions were overlooked in your assessment." This approach allows you to address the criticism without attacking the other person, keeping the conversation respectful and focused on resolving the issue.

- **Ask for Clarification: Seek specific examples for better understanding**

    Sometimes, criticism can be vague or ambiguous,

making it difficult to understand the specific issue at hand. In such cases, it's important to ask for clarification. Politely request specific examples or details that can help you better grasp the concern. For instance, you might say, "Could you provide an example of when you felt my work didn't meet expectations?" By seeking clarification, you demonstrate a willingness to engage constructively with the feedback and gain a clearer understanding of how you can improve.

Criticism doesn't have to be a source of conflict; it can be an opportunity to learn and grow. By listening fully, responding calmly, and seeking clarification when needed, you can handle criticism in a way that is both assertive and productive. This approach not only helps you maintain your composure and self-respect but also fosters a more open and constructive dialogue with the person offering the criticism.

Ultimately, how you deal with criticism can strengthen your relationships, build your resilience, and enhance your ability to navigate challenging situations with confidence and grace. By applying these tips, you'll be better equipped to turn criticism into a positive force for growth in both your personal and professional life.

Reflective Question: How do you usually react to criticism? Are you a mirror breaker? How could you handle criticism more assertively?

Role-playing Exercises for Practice

Practicing through role-playing can significantly enhance your ability to handle real-life conflicts assertively.

- **Role-playing Scenario:** Imagine a coworker disagrees with your approach on a project. Practice how you would assertively address the disagreement, seek common ground, and propose a solution.

Conclusion: Mastering Assertive Conflict Resolution

Handling conflicts assertively is a vital skill for maintaining healthy, productive relationships, whether in the workplace, at home, or in social settings. Conflicts are normal, but how we choose to address them can make all the difference in the outcome. When approached with assertiveness, conflicts can be transformed from obstacles into opportunities for understanding, growth, and collaboration.

In this chapter, you've been introduced to a range of strategies and exercises designed to help you navigate conflicts with confidence and integrity. From learning how to express your needs clearly, to negotiating and finding compromises, to dealing with criticism in a constructive manner, these tools empower you to address disagreements in a way that respects both your own boundaries and the perspectives of others.

As you continue to practice and refine these skills, you'll find that conflicts become less daunting and more manageable. You'll develop the ability to stay calm under pressure, communicate effectively even in challenging situations, and reach resolutions that are both fair and satisfying.

Remember, the goal of assertive conflict resolution is not just to resolve the immediate issue, but to build and maintain relationships that are based on mutual respect and understanding. With the strategies from this chapter in your toolkit, you're well on your way to mastering the art of handling conflicts with assertiveness and grace.

Reflective Question: What conflict are you currently facing that could benefit from these assertive techniques?

In Practice: Key Steps for Handling Conflicts Assertively

1. **Practice "Carefrontation"**

   Approach conflicts with care by focusing on resolving issues rather than placing blame. Express your needs calmly, using respectful language that prioritizes understanding over "winning" the argument.

2. **Prepare before the conversation**

   Take a few minutes to clarify your thoughts and goals before entering a conflict discussion. Knowing what you want to achieve can help you stay focused and reduce emotional reactions during the conversation.

3. **Use assertive language to communicate your perspective**

   Clearly express your viewpoint using "I" statements (e.g., "I feel…" or "I'd like…"). This keeps the focus on your experience and avoids triggering defensiveness in the other person.

4. **Listen to understand, not just to respond**

   Actively listen to the other person's perspective without interrupting. This shows respect and helps you gain valuable insight into their needs and feelings, which is essential for finding common ground.

5. **Suggest compromises where possible**

   Be open to finding a middle ground that addresses both parties' needs. Flexibility and willingness to compromise show that you value the relationship and are committed to a fair resolution.

6. **Keep your emotions in check**

   Stay mindful of your tone and body language to prevent the conflict from escalating. Take a deep breath if emotions start to rise, and keep the conversation focused on resolving the issue at hand.

7. **Reflect and learn**

   After the conflict, reflect on what went well and

what could have been handled differently. Use each experience as a learning opportunity to improve your conflict resolution skills over time.

Handling conflict assertively helps build trust, mutual respect, and understanding in your relationships. By practicing these steps, you can approach disagreements with confidence, turning potential conflicts into opportunities for growth and connection.

Chapter 6

Making Your Mark

Standing Out Assertively at Work

"If you don't stand up for something, you will fall for anything."
— *Malcolm X*

What to Expect: In this chapter, you'll discover how to apply assertiveness in the workplace. From setting professional boundaries to dealing with difficult colleagues, you'll gain strategies to communicate clearly while fostering respect. Whether you're seeking a promotion or setting limits on your workload, these insights will empower you in your career.

Finding Her Voice: Jane's Story

Jane was on student placement in the HR department of a well-reputed company. Her responsibilities included coordinating interviews, scheduling, contacting candidates to confirm their attendance, and liaising with her manager to facilitate interviews. However, Jane was overwhelmed by the long list of candidates she was assigned. As a newcomer with no prior experience in this kind of role, she felt unprepared. Although Jane's manager assumed her university had provided sufficient training, she had received no formal guidance in her new position.

Each morning, Jane walked into the office with a growing sense of anxiety. Every time she picked up the phone to call candidates, she found herself hoping they wouldn't answer. She even prayed that no calls would come in from candidates asking questions. Instead of focusing on learning and gaining experience, Jane's energy was consumed by her desire to avoid any interaction that made her uncomfortable.

Her manager, believing Jane had received sufficient training at university, often asked if she was managing well. Each time, Jane forced a smile and nodded, silently thinking,

If I admit I'm struggling, they'll think I'm not fit for this. She'd try to reassure herself; *Maybe things will get easier tomorrow.* But as the days passed, Jane's confidence faded. Instead of growing in her role, she simply aimed to survive each day without making a mistake.

The key issues in Jane's situation include:

1. **Avoidance:** Rather than face the challenge, Jane avoided opportunities to engage with candidates, hoping to escape the discomfort.

2. **Refusing support:** Jane declined her manager's help, fearing that admitting difficulty would damage her reputation.

3. **Shifted focus:** Instead of learning valuable skills, Jane's goal became survival, losing sight of the opportunity for growth.

4. **Fear of failure:** Jane was consumed by the fear of making mistakes, which held her back from trying new tasks or stepping out of her comfort zone. Her focus on avoiding failure meant she wasn't open to learning from her experiences.

5. **Lack of self-advocacy:** Jane didn't speak up for herself or communicate her concerns to her manager. This lack of self-advocacy kept her stuck in a cycle of anxiety and prevented her manager from understanding the full extent of her struggles.

6. **Negative self-talk:** It's likely that Jane's internal dialogue contributed to her lack of confidence.

Telling herself that she couldn't handle the task, or that seeking help would make her look incompetent, deepened her anxiety and created a mental barrier to assertiveness.

7. **Imposter syndrome[5]:** Jane's belief that she wasn't prepared for the role, despite her qualifications, might suggest a form of imposter syndrome. She doubted her abilities and believed she didn't belong in the role, which added to her reluctance to seek guidance or take charge.

From Survival to Success

Jane's struggles reached a point where she became overwhelmed and emotionally drained. She realized that she would not finish her placement successfully unless she took support from her manager for guidance and training. However, her diffidence and nervousness pulled her from behind and prevented her from proactively reaching out to her manager. She needed some mental 'push' to see her goal clearly so as to generate a psychological drive to assert her position.

In our sessions, we worked on understanding the deeper issues that were holding Jane back. We explored her

---

[5] Imposter syndrome is a psychological phenomenon where individuals doubt their abilities, feel like a fraud, and believe they don't deserve their achievements, despite evidence of their competence or success. People with imposter syndrome often attribute their success to luck or external factors rather than their own skills, and they fear that others will eventually discover that they are not as capable as they seem.

self-perception as incompetent, her anxiety that kept her from seeking help, and her discomfort with the responsibilities she was assigned in the absence of proper induction and training.

The following strategies helped:

1. Recognizing and challenging Jane's negative self-talk
2. Building self-advocacy skills
3. Understanding her rights as a trainee
4. Role-playing conversations
5. Addressing her fear of judgment

The sessions gave her some clarity about her needs, challenges, and strategies to overcome her struggles. She scheduled a meeting with her manager to discuss her concerns and mentally prepared herself for the conversation.

Sitting across the desk, she felt her heart pounding as she began, "I really want to do well here, and I think some additional training would help me meet the team's goals." Her mind raced as she continued, *I hope this doesn't make me look incompetent. But I need to be honest if I'm ever going to feel confident here.*

Jane used "I" statements to express her feelings without placing blame. She clarified that her goal was to contribute effectively to the team and that additional guidance would help her perform well.

The outcome was very positive. Her manager was quite receptive, appreciated Jane's honesty, and agreed to provide the training that she needed. They also arranged for her to shadow a senior team member to gain more hands-on experience.

Assertiveness at Workplace

Like Jane, many of us can find ourselves in situations where we feel overwhelmed or hesitant to speak up. However, as Jane discovered through her journey, learning to assert yourself is not just helpful—it's essential for your growth and success at work.

Assertiveness is not just a valuable skill—it's a necessity. Whether you're aiming for career advancement, striving for effective team collaboration, or seeking greater personal job satisfaction, asserting yourself professionally can make all the difference.

Assertiveness in the workplace allows you to communicate your ideas clearly, set boundaries respectfully, and advocate for your own needs and the needs of your team. It empowers you to confidently handle difficult conversations, deal with office dynamics effectively, and ensure that your contributions are recognized and valued.

Reflective Question: Think about your current work environment. Do you feel that your voice is heard and respected?

Jane's experience underscores the significance of being assertive at work and handling scenarios with confidence. From a place of extreme anxiety, she transformed to narrate a successful story by applying assertive techniques. Her story testifies that you can develop assertiveness as a valuable skill as you strive to enhance your communication at work more effectively and expressively.

Here are some key techniques that you can apply in the workplace:

Key Techniques

- **Clear Communication: State your thoughts, feelings, and needs directly**

    Assertiveness is about direct and open communication. Be clear on your thoughts, feelings, and needs so there can be no misunderstandings about the message you want to convey.

So, instead of "I am not sure if this timeline works for me," an alternative is: "I need another two days to complete this task effectively." Words such as: not sure, I think, maybe, perhaps, etc. will show uncertainty and lack of confidence and clarity about what you need and the solution. This will confuse your boss even more, and they will be left scratching their heads, trying to find an easy way out for you in the workplace.

- **Assertive Emailing: Use precise language and be direct about your needs**

Being assertive in your emails is just as important as in face-to-face interactions. Use precise language and get straight to the point. Avoid vague or overly polite language that could dilute the message. For instance, instead of writing, "I was wondering if it might be possible to have the report by Friday," an assertive message is, "Please send the report by Friday so I can review it before our Monday meeting." This approach conveys your needs clearly and sets clear expectations, helping streamline communication and improve efficiency.

- **Meeting Participation: Speak up confidently using "I" statements**

Meetings are an essential part of workplace collaboration, and being assertive in meetings ensures that your ideas and opinions are heard. Practice using "I" statements to express your views confidently. For example, instead of saying, "We might want to consider another approach," try saying, "I believe another approach could be more effective because..." This not only makes your contribution clear but also shows that you take ownership of your ideas. Additionally, assertive participation in meetings demonstrates your engagement and commitment to the team's success, earning you greater respect and recognition from your colleagues.

By applying these techniques, you'll be able to communicate with greater clarity and confidence in your professional environment. As you develop these skills, you'll build stronger connections with colleagues, contribute more meaningfully to your team, and enjoy your career with greater ease and effectiveness.

Reflective Question: In your current role, how can you apply these assertiveness techniques to ensure your voice is heard in team discussions?

Setting Professional Boundaries

It's easy to overlook the importance of setting boundaries at work, or worse, assume they aren't needed. But without them, it's almost inevitable that things can spiral—leading to feeling overworked, stressed out, and ultimately less productive. Over the course of my career in mental health, I've seen boundaries blur in ways that create tension. Sometimes people take on tasks that aren't theirs, while others avoid responsibilities, assuming it's someone else's job. The reality is, without clear boundaries, miscommunication and burnout are just around the corner.

By setting boundaries, you're not only protecting your own time and energy, but you're also encouraging respect from your colleagues and supervisors. It's not about being rigid; it's about creating an environment where everyone knows what's expected.

Priya's Turning Point: Learning to Set Boundaries

When Priya, a recent immigrant from India, joined her new team in the U.S., she quickly became known as the go-to person for help. Her colleagues often turned to her for assistance with tasks outside her job description, and while she wanted to be supportive, the extra workload started affecting her well-being. Recognizing the need to set boundaries, Priya decided to speak up. The next time a coworker asked her to stay late for an additional project, she replied kindly, "I'm committed to finishing my main tasks well, so I'll need to pass on this one tonight."

Initially, Priya worried that her colleagues might view her differently, but they respected her response. Over time, her team members learned to approach her with more consideration, which allowed Priya to focus on her work without feeling overwhelmed. This boundary not only improved her productivity but also strengthened her relationship with her colleagues, who began to appreciate her dedication without taking advantage of her willingness to help.

When Good Intentions Cross Boundaries: My Story

When reflecting on my own experience with setting boundaries, I recall a pivotal moment early in my career. At that time, I saw a pressing need to streamline our processes for recording client details, managing appointments, session notes, and discharge summaries. With limited resources and a budding department, I took it upon myself to develop a software system over the course of three months. The response from my team was overwhelmingly positive; they appreciated the efficiency and ease it brought to their work.

However, this effort, rooted in genuine intention and dedication, unexpectedly led to a boundary challenge. A colleague, harboring different motives, filed a complaint with the General Manager, claiming that my initiative was outside my role description. They argued that such software development should have been the responsibility of the IT department, accusing me of overstepping professional boundaries. It was a difficult moment—my contribution, intended to improve workflow and efficiency, was weaponized against me.

This experience forced me to re-evaluate how and when to establish clear professional boundaries. It taught me that while initiative and innovation can be positive, they must be balanced with a clear understanding of one's role and responsibilities. Boundaries not only protect personal and professional integrity but also ensure clarity about what is within and beyond one's scope. This situation underscored the importance of defining limits, even when acting with good intentions, to protect oneself from unexpected backlash and maintain focus on one's primary responsibilities.

Steps to Set Boundaries

- **Know Your Limits: Understand what you can handle and communicate it**

    The first step in setting boundaries at work is recognizing your own limits. Take a moment to figure out what you can reasonably manage in terms of workload, availability, and personal commitments. Knowing your capacity will help you identify when you're starting to stretch yourself too thin.

    Once you're clear on your boundaries, it's essential to communicate them. You might say something like, "I'm available for meetings between 9 AM and 5 PM, but I'll need to focus on projects outside those hours." By being upfront, you set expectations early and avoid misunderstandings.

- **Stick to Your Boundaries: Be consistent**

    Establishing boundaries is one thing; maintaining them is another. Once you've communicated your limits, it's crucial to stick to them, even when you face pushback. This might involve gently reminding coworkers of your availability or making sure you don't compromise your work hours, even when pressured to do more. For example, if you've decided that weekends are your personal time, reinforce that by not checking work emails during those days. Consistency helps others respect your boundaries, and over time, it creates a more balanced work environment.

- **Learn to Say No: Decline what's beyond your capacity**

    One of the hardest parts of maintaining boundaries is learning how to say no. It's natural to want to be helpful, but constantly taking on more can lead to burnout. When a task or request exceeds your capacity, it's okay to turn it down, politely but firmly. For instance, you could say, "I'd love to help, but my plate is full right now, and I wouldn't be able to give this the attention it needs." Saying no doesn't mean you're being difficult; it means you're making sure the work you do take on gets done well, without overextending yourself.

Setting boundaries isn't just about managing time—it's about ensuring you can do your best work and still take care of yourself. When you know your limits, maintain them, and say no when necessary, you're creating a work environment that supports your well-being and productivity. As you practice these skills, they'll become a natural part of your routine, allowing you to thrive both at work and in your personal life.

Reflective Question: Where in your work life could setting boundaries help you feel more balanced and in control?

Dealing with Difficult Colleagues

Interactions with challenging colleagues or supervisors can be one of the most stressful aspects of a professional environment. Whether you're dealing with a colleague who's consistently uncooperative or a manager who's overly critical, these situations can test your patience and professionalism. However, by approaching these interactions with assertiveness, you can manage these relationships more effectively, reducing stress and maintaining a positive work environment.

When Silence Isn't Golden: Facing Challenges with a Difficult Colleague

In my career, I've had my fair share of interactions with difficult colleagues, but one situation remains particularly memorable. There was a new member of the team who seemed to struggle with confidence in her own abilities and work. To deflect attention from her own shortcomings, she often turned the focus onto me in subtle yet undermining ways. It was her method of building her own standing within the team, often by spreading comments that cast doubt on my work or by publicly questioning my progress on certain tasks.

In team meetings, her approach became more pronounced. She would openly ask whether I had completed specific tasks, framing her questions in a way that suggested lapses on my end. Her intention was clear—she hoped to present herself as in control and aware while casting me in a less capable light. These questions weren't her responsibility to ask, and raising them publicly only served to create discomfort and tension.

At the time, I often chose to respond calmly, thinking it was better to diffuse potential conflict and keep the peace. But each response came with a cost. I found myself feeling smaller and more frustrated with every exchange, sacrificing my own sense of worth for the sake of maintaining superficial harmony. I was not truly protecting my mental health—instead, I was avoiding necessary confrontation.

Over time, I came to understand that my reluctance to assert my boundaries and address the situation directly had inadvertently fueled her behavior. By striving to maintain peace and avoid tension, I had allowed an unhealthy dynamic to persist. This experience showed me that dealing with challenging colleagues requires more than silence and tolerance—it demands a commitment to setting boundaries, standing up for oneself, and addressing behavior that erodes mutual respect and teamwork.

Strategies for Dealing with Difficult Individuals

Here are some strategies to help you deal with difficult individuals in a professional and assertive manner:

- **Stay Calm and Professional: Keep your emotions in check**

    When faced with a difficult colleague or manager, it's natural to feel frustrated, angry, or even intimidated. However, it's important to keep your emotions in check and respond calmly and professionally. Losing your temper or reacting emotionally can escalate the situation and potentially harm your reputation. Instead, take a deep breath, maintain a steady tone of voice, and focus on the facts. For example, if a colleague is being dismissive, you might say, "I understand your point of view, but I believe we should also consider this aspect..." Staying calm and composed demonstrates your professionalism and helps to de-escalate tense situations.

- **Focus on the Issue, Not the Person: Address behaviors and situations**

    One of the key principles of assertive communication is to focus on the issue at hand, rather than making it personal. When addressing a conflict or challenging behavior, concentrate on the specific actions or situations that need to be resolved, rather than attacking the individual's character. For instance, instead of saying, "You're always so negative," you could say, "I've noticed that during meetings, there's a lot of focus on the problems. I'd like us to also discuss potential solutions." This approach helps to keep the conversation constructive and prevents the individual from becoming defensive, which can lead to a more productive resolution.

- **Seek Mediation if Needed: Involve a third party for escalated conflicts**

    In some cases, despite your best efforts to handle the situation assertively, conflicts with difficult colleagues or managers may escalate beyond what you can manage on your own. When this happens, it's important to know when to seek help from a third party, such as HR or a mediator. Mediation can provide a neutral space where both parties can express their concerns and work towards a resolution. For example, you might approach HR and say, "I'm experiencing ongoing issues with a colleague that we haven't been able to resolve. I think it would be helpful to have a mediated conversation to find a solution." Seeking mediation shows that you're committed to resolving the conflict professionally and are willing to take the necessary steps to maintain a healthy work environment.

Dealing with difficult colleagues or managers is never easy, but by approaching these situations with assertiveness, you can protect your own well-being while also striving for a positive outcome. By staying calm, focusing on the specific issues, and knowing when to seek help, you can manage challenging relationships in a way that upholds your professionalism and integrity. These strategies will not only help you navigate difficult interactions more effectively but also contribute to a more respectful and productive workplace overall.

When Cultural Norms Collide: My Story

The popular notion that "first impressions are the best impressions" can sometimes work against you, especially when you're living and working in a different country. I learned this firsthand when I migrated to Ireland from my homeland, India.

I was raised in a traditional South Indian family, where making direct eye contact with elders or authority figures was considered impolite, confrontational, and disrespectful. Culturally, it was ingrained in me to show respect by averting my gaze. However, this well-intentioned behavior clashed with the cultural norms of my new environment, where maintaining eye contact is often perceived as a sign of confidence, trustworthiness, and engagement. Despite my inner confidence, I was often perceived at work as diffident, detached, and "not up to the standard" expected of my peers. It took time, discomfort, and deliberate effort to adapt. I had to train myself to maintain eye contact even when it felt unnatural, forcing myself to step outside the habits I had known all my life. Over time, I succeeded. Now, when I reflect on the experience, I often tell others that first impressions can be misleading. In my case, they led to misjudgment and significant emotional strain.

Another cultural barrier I encountered was related to speaking up in meetings. In my upbringing, speaking less and listening more was a virtue, a sign of thoughtfulness and respect. My instinct was to speak only when I felt it was truly necessary. However, this cultural trait didn't serve me well in a workplace environment where frequent participation and visible engagement in meetings often equate to competence and contribution. The contrast became evident when colleagues, who seemed to speak at every opportunity but didn't necessarily deliver as much in terms of tangible results, received recognition and praise. Meanwhile, my own hard work went largely unnoticed because I didn't speak up as often. It was an eye-opening realization that effective communication and assertiveness in this context required me not only to perform but to actively showcase my work and perspectives.

Adapting to a new culture comes with its challenges. It often forces us to confront deeply rooted behaviors and adopt new ways of connecting with others. While these cultural adjustments may be difficult, they can also be empowering. Learning to look someone in the eye, speak up confidently in meetings, and find my voice in new and unfamiliar ways have all helped me bridge cultural divides, assert my worth, and reshape how I'm perceived. And, as I learned, the first impression isn't always the lasting one—sometimes, the true story unfolds only with time, patience, and persistence.

Speak Up or Miss Out: Alex's Promotion Story

Alex had been working diligently for several years and felt that the time had come to take the next step in his career. His performance had consistently exceeded expectations, and he had taken on additional responsibilities that demonstrated his readiness for a leadership role. Confident in his achievements and contributions, Alex decided it was time to have a conversation with his manager about a promotion.

Understanding the importance of preparation and assertiveness in such discussions, Alex began by gathering evidence of his accomplishments. He compiled a detailed record of his successes, including completed projects, initiatives he had spearheaded, and the positive impact his work had on the company's goals. Alex knew that having concrete examples would strengthen his case and provide his manager with a clear picture of his value to the organization.

Once he felt prepared, Alex scheduled a meeting with his manager to discuss his career progression. Rather than waiting for an annual review or hoping for a promotion to be offered, Alex took the initiative to set up a dedicated time for this important conversation.

When the day of the meeting arrived, Alex approached it with calm confidence. He knew that assertive communication would be key to effectively conveying his readiness for a promotion. As he sat down with his manager, Alex began by thanking him for the opportunity to discuss his career development. He then transitioned into a clear and direct statement of his intentions.

"Based on my accomplishments over the past year and my ongoing commitment to the team and company, I believe I am ready to take on more responsibility as a team leader," Alex stated. He went on to highlight specific examples of his contributions, such as leading a successful project that had significantly increased revenue and mentoring junior colleagues who had since become high performers.

Alex's approach was assertive but respectful. He didn't demand a promotion, nor did he downplay his achievements. Instead, he presented his case with clarity and confidence, showing that he had thoughtfully considered his readiness for the next step in his career.

His manager, impressed by Alex's preparation and the direct yet professional way he communicated his request, responded positively. He acknowledged the impact of Alex's work and appreciated the initiative Alex had taken to discuss his career goals openly. The conversation led to a successful negotiation, with Alex's manager agreeing to support his promotion to team leader.

Alex's experience is a powerful example of how assertive communication can pave the way for career advancement. By preparing thoroughly, clearly articulating his achievements, and confidently stating his intentions, Alex was able to secure the promotion he had worked so hard for. His story illustrates the importance of taking control of your career development and the value of being proactive, prepared, and assertive in professional negotiations.

Conclusion: The Power of Assertiveness in Professional Success

Maya Angelou rightly said, *"You may not control all the events that happen to you, but you can decide not to be reduced by them."* Assertiveness can make you stand tall and speak clearly, set your priorities with confidence, give adequate respect to different perspectives, and set clear boundaries. You are advocating for yourself without compromising your values or beliefs. In that way, assertiveness is not just a communication tool; rather, it's a way to take control of your professional life while staying true to yourself.

"The boundary to what we can accept is the boundary to our freedom," said philosopher Tara Brach. When you know where your limits are, you give yourself the freedom to focus on what truly matters.

The ability to set boundaries is particularly vital in maintaining a healthy work-life balance. When you're clear about your limits and communicate them assertively, you protect your time, energy, and well-being, reducing the risk of burnout and enhancing your overall job satisfaction. Consistency in upholding these boundaries reinforces your professionalism and ensures that others respect your needs.

As you practice these skills, you'll see that assertiveness isn't just something you use in moments of conflict or during negotiations—it's a lifelong tool for professional growth. It's about making sure your career path aligns with your values and that you succeed on your own terms.

"Speak your mind, even if your voice shakes." Maggie Kuhn's words remind us that assertiveness isn't about being loud or forceful—it's about having the courage to stand up for yourself, even when it's hard.

Incorporating the strategies from this chapter into your daily work life will enable you to handle challenges with grace, communicate with clarity, and build stronger, more respectful relationships with your colleagues. Ultimately, assertiveness is about empowering yourself to take control of your professional journey while maintaining the respect and integrity that are crucial for long-term success.

Reflective Question: In what professional scenario could a more assertive approach improve your outcomes?

In Practice: Key Steps for Assertiveness in Professional Settings

1. **Set clear boundaries with colleagues and supervisors**

   Clearly communicate your availability and limits in a professional but friendly manner. For example, if you're given extra tasks, respectfully state your current workload and discuss priorities with your supervisor.

2. **Speak up in meetings and group discussions**

   Practice sharing your ideas confidently. If speaking up feels challenging, prepare a few points beforehand and look for moments to contribute. Assertive participation helps build your presence and credibility.

3. **Use "I" statements to address issues**

   If conflicts arise or feedback is needed, focus on "I" statements (e.g., "I've noticed…" or "I'd like…"). This approach keeps conversations constructive and minimizes misunderstandings.

4. **Request feedback proactively**

   Show your commitment to growth by asking for feedback on your performance. This demonstrates confidence and a willingness to learn, both essential for assertive professional development.

5. **Manage difficult conversations with diplomacy**

   Approach challenging discussions with a calm, solution-focused mindset. Reframe the conversation toward shared goals or problem-solving, which keeps interactions positive and professional.

6. **Acknowledge your achievements**

   Advocate for yourself by highlighting your contributions in a natural, confident way. Regularly sharing your successes—whether in meetings, reports, or performance reviews—demonstrates self-worth without sounding boastful.

7. **Handle criticism with confidence**

   Listen to feedback with an open mind and seek clarification if needed. Respond by acknowledging valid points and expressing how you plan to improve, showing both humility and a proactive attitude.

Applying these assertive strategies in the workplace can enhance your professional relationships, build your credibility, and foster a respectful, collaborative environment. Start by practicing one or two techniques to gradually strengthen your workplace communication skills.

Chapter 7

Bridging Hearts and Boundaries

Assertiveness in Personal Connections

"Seek first to understand, then to be understood." Stephen R. Covey

When it comes to personal life, it becomes even more challenging to say no to our dear ones. Even though we will be busy with our work-related schedules, we hate to say no to family members. So, the chances of being late for family demands, not fulfilling family commitments, etc., will be very high, resulting in relationship issues.

Assertiveness in personal relationships is about finding your voice and expressing your needs without fear of rejection or guilt. It's about fostering deeper connections built on honesty and mutual respect. As we explore this chapter, we'll look at practical ways to assert yourself in your personal life so you can build stronger, healthier relationships that honor both your needs and the needs of those you care about.

What to Expect: Here, we shift focus to personal relationships, showing how assertiveness can build stronger, more authentic connections. This chapter covers everything from setting boundaries with loved ones to expressing your needs without guilt. You'll learn to balance empathy and self-respect, helping you nurture healthier relationships.

Whether you're dealing with recurring issues, difficult conversations, or simply trying to ensure that your voice is heard, the tools and techniques discussed here will empower you to engage with your loved ones in a way that honors your own integrity and respect for them.

Reflective Question: Think about a recent personal interaction. Did you express your true feelings, or did you hold back? Why?

Maintaining Relationships While Being Assertive

Maintaining strong, healthy relationships while being assertive doesn't mean sacrificing the strength or warmth of those connections. When done thoughtfully, assertiveness can enhance your relationships, making them more open, honest, and resilient. The key is to communicate your needs and boundaries in a way that honors your feelings and those of your loved ones.

Below are some key techniques to help you maintain strong, supportive relationships while practicing assertiveness: your feelings and those of your loved ones.

Key Techniques

- **Express yourself openly and sincerely by sharing your thoughts and emotions.**

  Effective and honest communication forms the foundation of relationships, where being assertive involves sharing your thoughts and feelings directly while still being mindful of the person's feelings, striking a balance between expressing your needs truthfully without seeming harsh or inconsiderate. Instead of stating, "You never listen to me," you could express it as, "It makes me feel unheard when our discussions are constantly interrupted; I'm eager to find ways for us to communicate effectively." This approach allows you to address issues constructively without causing unnecessary hurt or tension.

- **Respect Differences: Recognize that differing opinions are OK with interactions.**

  No matter how close you are to someone, disagreements are bound to happen. Being assertive doesn't mean always agreeing or seeing things the same way as the other person. Instead, it involves recognizing that differences in opinion, values, or preferences are a normal part of any relationship. When disagreements arise, approach them with respect and understanding. Acknowledge the other person's perspective and express your own without judgment. For example, you might say, "I understand that you see it differently, but here's how I feel about it..." Such respectful dialogue can strengthen your relationship by fostering mutual respect and deeper understanding.

- **Balance Speaking and Listening: Ensure communication is a two-way street**

  Assertive communication isn't just about expressing yourself—it's also about being a good listener. To maintain strong relationships, it's essential to balance speaking and listening, ensuring that both parties feel heard and valued. When you speak, be clear and assertive about your needs, but also make space for the other person to share their thoughts and feelings. Listen actively, showing that you genuinely care about their perspective. This two-way communication builds trust and helps to prevent misunderstandings, leading to a more harmonious and connected relationship.

Maintaining relationships while being assertive is all about finding the right balance between expressing your needs and respecting the needs of others. By communicating openly and honestly, respecting differences, and ensuring that both parties have a voice, you can be assertive without compromising the warmth and strength of your personal connections. These techniques will help you navigate the complexities of personal relationships with grace and integrity, allowing you to build deeper, more meaningful bonds with those you care about.

Emma's Overcommitment to Her Friend

Emma prided herself on always being there for her friends. Whenever someone needed help, she was the first to say yes, even if it meant stretching herself thin. One weekend, her friend Lucy asked if Emma could help her plan a surprise birthday party for her husband. Emma had already committed to other plans, including a work deadline she had to meet, but not wanting to disappoint Lucy, she immediately said yes.

As the week went by, Emma became overwhelmed.

Between her job, family commitments, and the added pressure of planning the party, she found herself running out of time. She hadn't followed up on the venue or the catering as promised, and the day of the event was quickly approaching. The night before the party, Lucy called, excitedly asking about the final details. Emma panicked and had to admit she hadn't been able to get everything done.

Lucy was hurt. She had relied on Emma's promise and now, at the last minute, was left scrambling to fix everything. Emma felt terrible, knowing that she had let her friend down. Even though Lucy understood that Emma had been busy, the disappointment still hung between them. Their once easy-going friendship now felt strained, and Lucy hesitated to ask Emma for help in the future, fearing another letdown.

This situation made Emma realize the consequences of overcommitting. By saying yes when she couldn't truly follow through, she had unintentionally hurt her friend and created tension in their relationship. Emma learned that sometimes, it's better to say no with honesty than to say yes and fail to deliver.

Are these questions on your mind?

- *How can I say no to my friends and family?*
- *Am I obligated to say yes, even if it makes me uncomfortable?*
- *Do I have to agree, even if it doesn't feel right to me?*
- *Will saying no hurt my relationship with them?*

- *Should I just say yes, even if it makes things difficult for me?*

People have a genuine desire to avoid causing discomfort to others, and they don't want to risk hurting someone's feelings. Out of this desire, many end up saying yes when they truly want to say no, thinking it will protect the relationship. But in doing so, they may unintentionally underestimate the other person's capacity for kindness and understanding.

Remember, saying no can often be more supportive and honest than saying yes and bearing the burden yourself. When you set a boundary respectfully, you're honoring your own needs and encouraging mutual respect and understanding.

Think of this scenario: Clara is the kind of person who rarely says no to her family and friends. So when her best friend, Megan, asked her for help moving into a new apartment over the weekend, Clara agreed without a second thought. She had a big project due for work, but she figured she could squeeze everything in somehow. After all, she didn't want to let Megan down.

That weekend, Clara spent hours helping with boxes, lifting heavy furniture, and organizing Megan's new place. By the end of the day, she was exhausted and had barely touched her work. Late into the night, Clara tried to catch up, but the stress was building. The next day, she was tired, overwhelmed, and still far from finished with her project.

Break Free to Own Your Space

When Megan realized how much Clara had sacrificed to help, she felt a pang of guilt. She hadn't intended to burden Clara so much, and a part of her wished Clara had just been honest about her own commitments. Although Megan was grateful, she couldn't shake the feeling that she had caused her friend unnecessary stress. In the end, both friends felt a bit awkward about the whole situation—Clara felt drained, and Megan was left feeling guilty.

This story highlights the real impact of saying yes when it's a struggle. Clara's "yes" may have seemed easier in the moment, but in the end, it caused more difficulty than a gentle "no" would have. Setting boundaries isn't about letting others down; it's about being honest so everyone knows where they stand.

Steps to Say No Assertively

The story of Clara and Megan reminds us that saying yes when we're stretched too thin can lead to exhaustion, strain, and even guilt for those who asked for our help. Setting boundaries by saying no—politely but firmly—allows us to honor our own needs while maintaining respect for the other person. Here are some steps to help you say no confidently and kindly:

1. **Take a moment before responding**

   When someone asks for your help, pause before answering. A simple "Let me check my schedule" or "I'll need a moment to think about it" gives you the space to consider your own commitments and energy levels before making a decision.

2. **Express appreciation for the request**

   Acknowledging the person's need shows that you value the relationship. You might say, "Thanks for thinking of me" or "I appreciate you trusting me with this." This helps soften the response, showing respect for their request even if you can't fulfill it.

3. **Be clear and direct in your response**

   Avoid vague language that can lead to misunderstandings. A firm "I won't be able to help this time" is more effective than a hesitant "Maybe…" or

"I'll try." Directness conveys your limits respectfully without leaving room for confusion.

4. **Provide a brief reason, if appropriate**

   If it feels right, briefly explain why you're saying no. This helps the other person understand that it's about your capacity, not a lack of willingness. For example, "I'm focusing on a big work project this weekend and need the time to recharge."

5. **Suggest an alternative solution**

   Offering a different way to help, if possible, shows goodwill without overextending yourself. For instance, "I can't assist with the whole move, but I'd be happy to lend a hand for an hour" or "I can recommend someone else who may be able to help."

6. **Stand firm and resist pressure**

   If the person pushes back, it's okay to repeat your response. Politely reinforce your decision by saying, "I understand, but I truly can't take this on right now." Standing firm encourages respect for your boundaries over time.

7. **Express your continued support and care**

   Reaffirming your commitment to the relationship can ease any disappointment. Ending with "I'm here for you in other ways" or "Please reach out if you need anything else" maintains a supportive tone, showing that saying no doesn't mean withdrawing from the friendship or family connection.

By following these steps, you can say no in a way that respects your own needs without creating tension or guilt in your relationships. Assertive communication like this allows both you and your loved ones to grow in understanding, honesty, and mutual support.

Reflective Question: Is there a situation where you need to say no to someone close to you? How can you do it assertively?

Balancing Assertiveness and Empathy

Learning to say no assertively is essential, but there's an added layer that strengthens relationships even further: empathy. Balancing assertiveness with empathy means expressing your needs while also recognizing and valuing the emotions of others. When we lead with both qualities, we're able to protect our own well-being while showing care for the people we value. This approach builds trust, as people feel both respected and understood.

Emilio, whose family emigrated from Mexico to the U.S. when he was young, often felt a strong sense of duty to say "yes" to family requests. His cousin frequently asked him to help with errands on weekends, which left Emilio feeling frustrated, as he rarely had time to pursue his own activities. One weekend, he gathered the courage to express a boundary: "I'm happy to help when I can, but I need time for my own plans too. If we can schedule things in advance, I can see if I'm available."

Though he was nervous about how his cousin might react, Emilio was relieved when his cousin understood and agreed to plan ahead. This small change gave Emilio more control over his time, and he felt more appreciated within his family. By setting this boundary, Emilio strengthened his bond with his cousin, building a dynamic of respect and understanding in place of unspoken frustration.

Techniques for Balancing Assertiveness and Empathy

1. **Listen actively before responding**

    Empathy begins with listening. When someone shares a request or a concern, make sure you're fully present and engaged before responding. Show you're actively listening with nods, eye contact, and open body language. This gives them the space to feel heard, which can make setting boundaries easier and more respectful.

2. **Use "I" statements to convey your needs**

    Expressing your needs with "I" statements keeps the focus on your own feelings and experiences, rather than placing blame. For instance, say, "I feel overwhelmed with my current workload and need time to rest," rather than "You're asking too much of me." This approach respects both your needs and the other person's emotions.

3. **Acknowledge their feelings**

   When setting a boundary, take a moment to recognize the other person's feelings. You might say, "I know this is important to you" or "I understand that this means a lot." This simple acknowledgment shows you're not dismissing their needs, even if you can't meet them.

4. **Show appreciation for their understanding**

   After setting a boundary, express gratitude for their understanding. A small phrase like "Thanks for being open to my perspective" or "I appreciate you understanding where I'm coming from" reinforces a sense of mutual respect. It lets them know their willingness to honor your needs matters to you.

5. **Offer an alternative, if possible**

   If it's appropriate, suggest a compromise or an alternative that respects both of your needs. For instance, if a friend asks for your time but you're busy, you might say, "I can't meet this weekend, but I'd love to catch up next week." Offering an alternative helps maintain connection while preserving your boundaries.

6. **Practice compassionate honesty**

   Being honest doesn't mean being blunt. Choose words that convey your message thoughtfully. For example, instead of saying "I'm too busy to deal with this," try "I have a lot on my plate, and I want to give this my full attention when I can." Compassionate honesty shows that you're being genuine without disregarding their feelings.

7. **Use a soft tone and open body language**

   Tone and body language go a long way in communicating empathy. A calm, steady voice and open posture make it easier for the other person to accept your message without feeling hurt. Avoid crossed arms or a sharp tone, which might come across as defensive or dismissive.

   Balancing assertiveness with empathy allows you to set healthy boundaries while building trust and understanding. By using these techniques, you can communicate your needs clearly and kindly, creating a space where both you and others feel respected and valued.

Julia's Family Gathering

The value of balancing assertiveness with empathy can be seen in personal situations, like the one Julia faced with her family. Julia loved her family gatherings. They were always full of laughter, connection, and the joy of catching up with her loved ones. So, when her family planned a big gathering for the upcoming weekend, she felt torn. She had already set that time aside for rest—a break she knew she needed after weeks of exhaustion.

In the past, Julia might have pushed her own needs aside and agreed to go, worried about disappointing her family. But this time, she decided to approach things differently. She'd been working on speaking up for her needs while still being considerate of others, and this felt like the perfect chance to put that skill into practice.

Instead of agreeing right away and then quietly resenting the loss of her downtime, Julia chose to have an open conversation with her family. She started by letting them know how much their time together meant to her. "I love our family gatherings and look forward to them," she said, making it clear that her feelings hadn't changed. Then she shared her own need for rest, saying, "I've just been feeling worn out lately and was hoping to use this weekend to recharge."

Julia's family listened. And because she spoke with honesty and kindness, they understood her perspective and didn't feel let down. In fact, they appreciated her honesty and suggested a different plan—a smaller, more casual get-together that would allow her to relax and still see everyone.

The scaled-down gathering turned out to be a perfect solution. Julia enjoyed time with her family without feeling drained, and the experience reinforced how valuable it can be to balance assertiveness with empathy. By expressing her needs openly, Julia showed her family that caring for herself didn't mean neglecting them. This experience showed her that setting boundaries can actually bring people closer together.

Julia's story is a reminder that with the right approach, you don't have to choose between looking after yourself and keeping close relationships strong. Sometimes, it's all about finding that balance.

Building Assertiveness in Relationships

Bringing assertiveness into your personal relationships allows you to build a foundation of trust and respect. Being assertive doesn't mean always pushing for what you want; it means learning to communicate openly about your needs while respecting the other person's point of view. When approached with honesty and empathy, assertiveness can make relationships feel more genuine and balanced.

In this chapter, we explored some practical ways to be assertive with loved ones—whether it's finding a way to say no when necessary, staying true to your needs, or tackling tough conversations. Each of these techniques can help you create stronger, healthier connections that support both you and those around you.

As you try out these skills, you may find that relationships become more open and easier to navigate. Assertiveness, after all, is about creating space for real communication and mutual understanding. Over time, this approach can transform your connections, bringing both clarity and kindness into the relationships that matter most to you.

Sample Dialogues for Setting Family Boundaries

Example 1: Politely Declining a Family Request Without Guilt

Situation: Your sibling frequently asks you to help with last-minute errands, but you're already balancing a tight schedule.

Script: "[Sibling's name], I understand you're in a pinch, and I want to help when I can. Right now, though, my schedule is really packed, and I won't be able to make it. If we can plan a bit ahead next time, I'd love to help out when I'm free."

Why this works: You're showing understanding and willingness to help in the future, but you're also clearly prioritizing your own schedule.

Example 2: Addressing a Repeated Boundary Violation

Situation: A close family member repeatedly drops by unannounced, which disrupts your routine.

Script: "I love spending time with you, and it means a lot that you want to stop by. Lately, though, I've been really focused on my schedule, so it would help me a lot if we could plan visits in advance. That way, I can make sure I'm ready to enjoy our time together."

Why this works: You acknowledge the family member's intentions positively but set a clear boundary by asking for planned visits instead.

Example 3: Declining a Financial Request with Sensitivity

Situation: A family member asks for financial support, but you're not comfortable with lending money.

Script: "[Family member's name], I understand that things are challenging right now, and I really want the best for you. At the moment, though, I'm not in a position to help financially. I'm here for you in other ways, though—let me know if there's anything else I can do."

Why this works: This response is empathetic but firm, and it offers other types of support that might still be helpful.

In Practice: Key Steps for Assertiveness in Personal Relationships

1. **Express your feelings honestly**

    Use "I" statements to share your feelings with loved ones without placing blame. For example, "I feel hurt when…" or "I need…" keeps the focus on your experience, creating a more open and empathetic conversation.

2. **Set clear boundaries and stick to them**

    Whether it's about personal time, responsibilities, or emotional limits, assertively communicate your boundaries. For example, let others know if you need some quiet time to recharge or if there are topics you prefer not to discuss.

3. **Respect others' boundaries as well**

   Practicing assertiveness also means respecting the boundaries others set. Acknowledge their needs and avoid pressuring them to change their boundaries, which fosters mutual respect in relationships.

4. **Say "No" when needed without guilt**

   Politely decline requests that don't align with your priorities or capacity, using phrases like, "I won't be able to help this time." Saying "no" without guilt shows self-respect and honesty with those around you.

5. **Listen actively and validate others' feelings**

   Assertive communication isn't only about speaking up; it's also about listening fully. Validate others' emotions and perspectives, showing that you respect their experience and value open dialogue.

6. **Address conflicts calmly and openly**

   If disagreements arise, approach them with a calm and solution-oriented mindset. Express your perspective clearly, ask questions to understand the other person's view, and work together toward a resolution that respects both sides.

7. **Regularly communicate your needs**

   Assertive relationships are built on open, ongoing communication. Practice sharing your needs and preferences regularly to prevent misunderstandings and create a foundation of trust and respect.

By practicing assertiveness in your personal relationships, you create a healthy environment where both you and your loved ones feel respected and understood. Start with small steps, and watch your relationships grow stronger and more fulfilling.

Reflective Question: What steps can you take to become more assertive in your relationships while maintaining harmony?

Chapter 8

Breaking Free

Overcoming Fears and Roadblocks

"Obstacles don't have to stop you. If you run into a wall, don't turn around and give up. Figure out how to climb it, go through it, or work around it." — Michael Jordan

Becoming more assertive can feel empowering, but it's not always simple. When you've spent years communicating in certain ways, shifting to an assertive style may seem a bit daunting. Old habits are persistent, and the fear of conflict or disappointing others can make these changes harder to stick with.

What to Expect: This chapter acknowledges common hurdles, such as fear of conflict, rejection, or guilt. You'll find strategies to tackle these challenges and tips for managing setbacks. By understanding and addressing these obstacles, you'll be better prepared to stay consistent in your journey toward assertiveness.

It's easy to feel nervous about speaking up or uncomfortable with being direct, especially if those things are new to you. Yet, recognizing these feelings is a big step forward—each one of them is part of the journey and can be worked through gradually.

Here, we'll look at practical ways to face these

challenges. By understanding what holds you back, you can create a plan for moving forward, step by step. This chapter offers simple strategies to help you feel more comfortable expressing your needs and boundaries while building confidence in how you communicate.

Remember, assertiveness is something you build over time. Every small effort brings you closer to a balanced approach where you can express yourself openly and respectfully. Let's explore these common obstacles and look at ways to work through them, helping you strengthen your communication in every part of life.

Reflective Question: What are the main challenges you face when trying to be assertive?

Facing Common Fears and Moving Past Them

For many people, the idea of becoming more assertive stirs up a mix of emotions—often with some specific worries front and center. There might be a fear of conflict, concerns about being rejected, or even the thought that you might end up hurting someone's feelings. These are real and understandable feelings that can make it tough to find a middle ground in how you communicate. Sometimes, these worries can steer us toward staying too quiet or, on the other hand, coming across too strong. But learning to recognize and work through these fears is a key part of building assertiveness.

Below, we'll look at some of these common worries and share a few ideas for approaching them in a healthy, balanced way:

Fear of Conflict: Looking at Disagreements as Opportunities

One of the most common fears associated with assertiveness is the fear of conflict. The thought of disagreeing with someone, especially in a personal or professional setting, can be intimidating. Many people avoid assertiveness altogether because they fear that standing up for themselves will lead to confrontation or tension.

However, it's important to recognize that conflict, when handled constructively, is often a necessary part of reaching resolutions and fostering growth. Rather than seeing conflict as something to be feared, try to view it as an opportunity to address issues, find solutions, and deepen understanding.

How to Overcome It: Start by practicing conflict scenarios with a trusted friend, coach, or even in front of a mirror. Role-playing these situations can help you become more comfortable with the idea of conflict and teach you how to navigate disagreements assertively and calmly. Remind yourself that assertive conflict resolution is about finding common ground and achieving a positive outcome, not about "winning" the argument.

Fear of Rejection: Building Confidence Through Small Steps

It's normal to worry about rejection; for many of us, the thought of being dismissed or not receiving approval can make it hard to speak up for what we need or believe. This fear can lead to holding back, staying quiet, and ultimately not sharing who we really are.

One way to start moving past this is by slowly building resilience—gradually exposing yourself to moments where rejection could happen, but in a manageable way. Each time you face these situations, they begin to lose a bit of their hold over you.

How to Overcome It: Start with small, achievable goals that might involve a little risk of rejection. Maybe ask a coworker for a small favor or gently share a different opinion in a friendly conversation. If rejection happens, take a few moments to reflect on it—notice how it felt, what you learned, and think about how you'll approach it next time. Little by little, these experiences can help build a stronger sense of confidence, making it easier to stand up for yourself when bigger situations come along.

Fear of Hurting Others: Balancing Your Needs with Kindness

One big hurdle when it comes to being assertive is worrying about upsetting or hurting someone else. The idea of expressing your needs or setting boundaries can make you nervous, especially if you're concerned that it'll come across as harsh. This fear often makes you hold back, putting others' wants before your own.

But being assertive doesn't mean being unkind or dismissive. It's more about being clear about what you need, while still showing you respect the other person's feelings.

How to Approach It: Pay attention to the words you use when speaking up. Simple phrases like "I feel" or "I need" can help get your message across without sounding like you're accusing or blaming. For example, instead of saying, "You always cut me off," try something like, "I feel unheard when I get interrupted, and I'd love it if we could both have time to share." This lets you be honest but gentle.

Working through this takes time, but each small step can help you feel more comfortable speaking up for yourself. Over time, assertiveness will feel less like a hurdle and more like a natural way to communicate.

Reflective Question: Which of these fears do you connect with the most, and what's one thing you can try to start addressing it?

Dealing with Setbacks

Like any new skill, learning to be assertive will have its ups and downs. You might walk away from certain conversations thinking, "Well, that didn't go as planned." It's normal. Setbacks happen, and they're a big part of the learning process. Instead of feeling discouraged, try viewing these moments as chances to grow.

Let's look at a few ways to handle setbacks and keep building confidence as you work on assertiveness:

Strategies for Handling Setbacks

- **Reflect and Learn: Seeing setbacks as opportunities**

    After a setback, it can be helpful to take a step back and think about what happened. What was going on? How did you react? Reflecting this way, you learn from these moments so that you can find new approaches next time.

    How to use it: After a setback, try to carve out a quiet moment to think about what happened. Ask yourself questions like, "What could I have done differently?" or "How might I handle something similar in the future?" Even jotting down a few thoughts can be helpful. Over time, you might start seeing patterns that guide you forward.

- **Get Feedback: Fresh perspectives can be eye-opening**

    Sometimes it's hard to notice our own patterns. Asking for input from friends or trusted colleagues can help. They might spot something you missed or offer tips to help you fine-tune your approach.

    How to use it: After a challenging conversation, reach out to someone you trust. Say, "I'm working on being more assertive—do you have any thoughts on how I handled that?" Take their feedback to heart and consider how you might apply it next time. A fresh set of eyes can be precious.

- **Keep Practicing: Progress takes time**

    Assertiveness isn't something that changes overnight. The more you practice, the easier it'll feel. Setbacks will happen, but with each try, you're building confidence.

    How to use it: Start by practicing assertiveness in situations that feel manageable. Maybe it's setting a boundary or clearly expressing a need. As you build confidence, tackle bigger situations. And remember to celebrate the small wins—they're all steps toward the bigger goal.

Setbacks are simply part of learning. By reflecting on each experience, seeking outside input, and keeping at it, you'll find your voice getting stronger and clearer over time. Just keep at it—persistence is what makes progress.

Maintaining Assertiveness Under Pressure

Staying assertive in high-pressure situations is one of the most challenging aspects of assertive communication. Whether it's a tense meeting at work, a heated discussion with a loved one, or a moment of unexpected confrontation, the ability to remain assertive requires both preparation and a strong presence of mind. In these moments, it's easy to fall back to old habits—whether that's becoming overly passive or reacting aggressively. However, with the right techniques, you can maintain your assertiveness even when the stakes are high.

Here are some key techniques to help you stay assertive under pressure:

Techniques for Staying Assertive

- **Prepare Responses: Anticipate challenges and plan ahead**

One of the best ways to maintain assertiveness in high-pressure situations is to prepare in advance. If you know that a particular conversation or event might be challenging, take some time to anticipate potential conflicts or difficult questions. Preparing assertive responses ahead of time can give you the confidence to stay calm and clear-headed when the moment arrives.

How to Apply It: Consider the specific challenges you might face and rehearse how you will respond. For example, if you're heading into a meeting where you expect pushback on your ideas, practice stating your points assertively and preparing counterarguments. This preparation will help you feel more in control, reducing the likelihood of being caught off guard and reverting to less assertive behaviors.

- **Practice Stress Management: Stay composed with deep breathing and mindfulness**

High-pressure situations often trigger stress responses, making it harder to think clearly and communicate effectively. Practicing stress management techniques can help you maintain your composure and stay assertive, even when you're feeling anxious or overwhelmed. Deep breathing, mindfulness, and other relaxation techniques can calm your nervous system and keep you grounded in the moment.

How to Apply It: Before entering a stressful situation, take a few moments to center yourself. Practice deep breathing—inhale slowly and deeply through your nose, hold for a few seconds, and then exhale slowly through your mouth. This simple technique can help lower your heart rate and reduce anxiety. Additionally, practicing mindfulness—focusing on the present moment without judgment—can help you stay calm and focused, making it easier to respond assertively rather than react impulsively.

- **Use Assertive Body Language: Project confidence through your posture and gestures**

Your body language plays a crucial role in how assertive you appear, especially in high-pressure situations. Even if you're feeling nervous, maintaining assertive body language can help you project confidence and stay in control of the conversation. Open gestures, steady eye contact, and confident posture not only convey assertiveness to others but also reinforce it within yourself.

How to Apply It: In moments of pressure, be mindful of your body language. Keep your shoulders back, stand or sit up straight, and avoid crossing your arms, which can signal defensiveness. Make eye contact with the person you're speaking to, and use open hand gestures to emphasize your points. These non-verbal cues will help you communicate more effectively and assertively, even when you're under stress.

Maintaining assertiveness under pressure is a skill

that can be developed with practice and preparation. By anticipating challenges, managing your stress, and using assertive body language, you can navigate high-pressure situations with confidence and clarity. These techniques will not only help you stay true to your assertive communication style but also ensure that you handle even the most challenging interactions with poise and professionalism.

Remember, staying assertive under pressure is about preparation, presence of mind, and self-awareness. The more you practice these techniques, the more natural and effective they will become, allowing you to maintain your assertiveness in any situation.

Tom's Boardroom Challenge: Learning to Speak Up

Tom, a manager who always put his best into his work, found himself fading into the background during executive meetings. He had plenty of ideas but felt hesitant to share them, worried that he might come off too strong or overstep his boundaries. After a while, he started feeling frustrated, wondering if he was missing out on opportunities by staying quiet.

Tom decided it was time to change that. He looked into assertive communication and learned something surprising: being assertive wasn't about dominating the room but about sharing thoughts with clarity and respect.

For the next meeting, Tom did things differently. He

jotted down his main points, thought about possible questions, and practiced speaking with a steady tone. He focused on staying clear and calm, ready to make his points without overwhelming anyone.

When the meeting came, Tom felt a little nervous but also prepared. He waited for his moment, then spoke up, making sure to keep his tone steady and his message straightforward. To his surprise, his colleagues listened, nodding along and even asking questions.

That meeting marked a turning point for Tom. Each time he practiced speaking up, it got easier. Over time, he became a more active part of these discussions, gaining confidence and respect from his peers.

Tom's story shows how a shift in approach—plus a bit of practice—can make all the difference. Learning to speak up with respect for himself and others helped him find his voice in the workplace.

Conclusion: Growing Assertiveness One Step at a Time

Building assertiveness is something that takes time, practice, and a bit of patience. It means facing those common worries we all have—like the fear of upsetting someone, dealing with conflict, or worrying about how others might react. Recognizing these fears is an important first step toward managing them and learning to communicate with more confidence.

Throughout this chapter, we explored a few ways to help with these challenges. From preparing yourself for those tough conversations to handling setbacks and learning as you go, each tool is here to help you communicate clearly and stay true to yourself.

Remember, setbacks are natural. Every time you reflect on a difficult situation or learn from a conversation that didn't go as planned, you're getting stronger and more comfortable with speaking up. Over time, assertiveness will start to feel like a part of who you are.

In the end, assertiveness is about much more than just speaking up. It's about respecting yourself and your needs while considering those around you. Each small step counts, and with practice, being assertive will become second nature.

Reflective Question: What's one small action you can take today to start building your assertiveness?

In Practice: Key Steps for Overcoming Challenges to Assertiveness

1. **Identify your personal barriers**

   Reflect on what holds you back from being assertive. Is it fear of conflict, a desire to please others, or discomfort with setting boundaries? Recognizing these barriers is the first step to overcoming them.

2. **Challenge negative thoughts**

   Replace limiting beliefs (like "If I speak up, I'll seem

selfish") with supportive affirmations, such as "Expressing my needs is healthy and respectful." Positive self-talk reinforces your right to be heard.

3. **Practice assertiveness in low-stakes situations**

   Build confidence by practicing assertiveness in smaller, less intimidating settings. Start by expressing your opinion or setting a boundary with friends or family, and gradually work up to more challenging situations.

4. **Visualize assertive outcomes**

   Picture yourself handling difficult conversations assertively and with ease. Visualization can help you feel more prepared and confident when the actual situation arises.

5. **Accept that assertiveness takes practice**

   Embrace that setbacks are part of the learning process. If you fall back into old habits, be gentle with yourself and use the experience to refine your approach next time.

6. **Celebrate small wins**

   Acknowledge every step forward, no matter how small. Each time you assert yourself, you're building a stronger foundation for confident communication, so give yourself credit for your efforts.

7. **Seek support when needed**

   Don't hesitate to seek support from friends,

mentors, or even a counselor. Having someone to discuss your progress with can provide encouragement and fresh perspectives on handling challenges.

Overcoming challenges to assertiveness is a journey of self-growth. By practicing these steps, you'll build resilience, confidence, and the skills needed to communicate authentically, even in difficult situations.

Conclusion

Own Your Journey!

Building on Your Newfound Strength

"It always seems impossible until it's done." Nelson Mandela

Now that you're here at the end. Let's take a moment to appreciate how far you've come. You've learned ways to communicate clearly, set boundaries that feel right, and build honest connections. Assertiveness is all about respecting both yourself and others.

In this last chapter, we'll pull together all the insights from each section. Moving forward, these tools will be there to support you. You're building confidence in a way that fits you. Each small change adds up, and the journey keeps going from here.

What to Expect: As you complete this journey, this chapter helps you consolidate your learning and apply assertiveness consistently. You'll reflect on your progress and set actionable goals for the future. Remember, assertiveness is a skill you'll continue to develop—each step builds confidence, resilience, and respect in every area of life.

Embracing Your Assertive Journey

By now, you've navigated the ups and downs that come with learning new ways to communicate. Maybe it was facing a fear of conflict, managing stress in high-stakes situations, or bouncing back from those moments that didn't go as planned. Each step you took and each technique you tried brought you closer to making assertiveness a real part of who you are.

This journey wasn't just about picking up techniques. It was also about seeing your own voice in a new light—recognizing that it's worth being heard and respected. Assertiveness, at its heart, is about building honest connections that respect everyone involved, whether that's in your workplace, with family, friends, or in any part of life.

As you reflect, take a moment to appreciate the progress you've made. The insights and tools you've gained are meant to stick with you and support you through the challenges and successes still to come. Being assertive brings ease and confidence that can enrich both personal and professional aspects of life.

And remember, this is a journey without a finish line. Growing in assertiveness isn't something that happens all at once. It's a skill that you'll keep building, one that calls for patience and steady practice. Each time you apply what you've learned, you're growing in confidence and staying true to yourself, all while honoring those around you.

Your voice has value, and it deserves to be heard. Celebrate each small step you've taken, and look forward to all that lies ahead. Assertiveness is now a part of you, helping you shape your future, nurture your relationships, and live a life that feels balanced and fulfilling.

Reflecting on What You've Learned

As you come to the close of this journey, take a moment to look back on the changes you've begun to create. The steps you've taken toward assertiveness go beyond learning new ways to communicate—they represent a shift in how you see yourself and how you show up in the world. Here are some key areas to think about as you reflect on what you've gained:

Self-Awareness: Seeing Your Growth and Potential

It all started with building self-awareness. By taking an honest look at your communication style, you gained insights into how you interact with others and where you want to grow. Whether you noticed a tendency toward being too passive or too aggressive, this awareness has been a starting point for real change. Now, you're more tuned into those moments when you might hold back or react too strongly, and you're making intentional choices to communicate in a way that feels true to you. This level of awareness will keep supporting your personal and professional journey.

Skill Development: Putting Essential Techniques into Practice

Throughout this process, you've practiced key techniques that are already shaping how you communicate. You've learned to use "I" statements, helping you share your feelings without blame and making it easier to have open, respectful conversations. Setting and holding boundaries has also been a big part of this journey, allowing you to meet your own needs while respecting the needs of others. You've worked on handling conflicts with a focus on resolution rather than confrontation. Each skill has added to your growing confidence and effectiveness in expressing yourself.

Empowerment: Building Confidence to Express Your Needs

One of the most important shifts has been the confidence you've gained. Now, you're equipped to clearly express your needs, emotions, and boundaries, fostering respect and understanding in your relationships. This empowerment goes beyond simply speaking up; it's about valuing your own voice and ensuring it's heard in a way that reflects who you are and honors those around you. As you keep using these skills, you'll find this sense of empowerment reaching into many areas of life, changing how you see yourself and interact with others.

Looking back on what you've learned, you can see that the transformation has only just started. You're building a foundation for a more authentic, assertive, and empowered self. The self-awareness, skills, and confidence you've gained are more than just milestones—they're tools that will help you create a more balanced and fulfilling life. As you move forward, keep reflecting on these lessons, practicing these skills, and welcoming the growth that comes with being truly assertive. This journey is only beginning.

Reflective Question: How has your view of assertiveness shifted since starting this book?

Continuing Your Journey: Embracing Growth

Reaching the last page of this book doesn't mean the journey toward assertiveness is over. Becoming more assertive is an ongoing process—something that grows and changes with you over time. It's not about reaching a final goal; it's about learning a way of communicating that feels true to who you are. Keeping up with this practice takes patience, persistence, and a willingness to keep learning.

Here are some helpful ways to stay on track and let your assertiveness skills keep growing.

Keep Practicing: Make Assertiveness Part of Your Routine

The more you practice assertiveness, the more natural it becomes. The techniques you've learned, like using "I" statements, setting boundaries, or handling conflicts calmly, are tools that become sharper with use. When you practice these skills daily, assertiveness moves from being something you have to think about to something that comes more naturally.

How to Apply It: Look for everyday moments to use these skills. It could be sharing your opinion in a conversation, setting a boundary with a friend, or calmly speaking up in a group. The more often you integrate assertiveness into your daily life, the more natural it becomes.

Seek Feedback: Use Constructive Criticism to Grow

Getting feedback can be incredibly helpful for building assertiveness. Talk to friends, family, or colleagues who can give you honest insights about how you come across. Constructive feedback can show you where to improve and let you know what's working well in your approach.

How to Apply It: After an important conversation or decision, ask for feedback. You could say, "I'm working on assertive communication—how did I come across in that conversation?" Listen openly to their responses, and use what they share to keep refining your skills. Remember, feedback is for growth, not judgment.

Join Support Groups: Find a Safe Space to Practice

Learning alongside others on a similar journey can be very motivating. Joining a support group or workshop focused on assertiveness can give you a safe, supportive place to practice and learn. These groups offer a sense of community and the chance to learn from other's experiences and insights.

How to Apply It: Look for local or online groups focused on assertiveness, personal growth, or communication skills. These communities often offer role-playing, discussions, and workshops that let you try out what you've learned. Practicing in a supportive space with people on a similar path can boost your confidence and give you fresh perspectives.

As you continue this journey, remember that assertiveness is a skill that grows over time. It's not about being perfect; it's about sticking with it, learning from each experience, and communicating in a way that feels true to you. Practice regularly, welcome feedback, and find community support to keep building on what you've achieved.

Your journey is unique, and each step you take adds to your confidence and sense of self. Keep moving forward, be patient with yourself, and embrace the process. This journey toward assertiveness is one of the most empowering paths you can choose.

Moving Forward with Confidence

You've come a long way on this journey. Think back to the start, to the story I shared about my own struggle with people-pleasing, dealing with difficult colleagues, and addressing boundary issues at the workplace. It took time, practice, and persistence, but each step helped me move closer to speaking up for myself. It wasn't an instant transformation, but with each small choice, I began to build a life that felt more true to me.

Your path will be similar. Some days, using these skills might feel like second nature; other days, it might be more of a stretch. That's okay. Every time you choose to try, even if it's not perfect, you're strengthening your voice. Assertiveness is about making that choice moment by moment.

Each interaction from here on is a chance to keep practicing. Over time, these moments will add up to real change. Before you know it, assertiveness will feel like part of who you are.

Learning to be assertive has given me more peace, confidence, and honesty in my relationships. My hope is that it will do the same for you. Take pride in every step forward, trust in your progress, and remember—each effort matters.

Reflective Question: What will be your first step in continuing to develop your assertiveness after finishing this book?

In Practice: Key Steps for Continuing Your Assertiveness Journey

1. **Reflect regularly on your progress**

   Set aside time to review your experiences with assertiveness. Ask yourself what's working well and where you might need further growth. This reflection reinforces progress and helps you stay focused on your goals.

2. **Integrate assertiveness into daily interactions**

   Make assertiveness a regular habit by practicing it in everyday scenarios, from small requests to casual conversations. The more often you use these skills, the more natural they'll become.

3. **Use setbacks as learning opportunities**

   When challenges arise, don't be discouraged. Instead, view setbacks as valuable lessons that reveal areas for improvement. Each experience offers insights that strengthen your assertiveness.

4. **Revisit key techniques as needed**

   Periodically return to the techniques covered in this book—like "I" statements, active listening, and setting boundaries. Reviewing these tools helps keep your skills sharp and adaptable to new situations.

5. **Stay mindful of your boundaries and needs**

Continue to check in with yourself about your personal boundaries and needs, and communicate them openly. Staying mindful of these will help you maintain self-respect and balance in all relationships.

6. **Celebrate each success**

   Acknowledge every time you assert yourself, no matter how small the situation. Recognizing and celebrating these moments reinforces your progress and builds confidence.

7. **Commit to lifelong growth**

   Remember that assertiveness is a lifelong skill that will continue to evolve. Keep learning, adapting, and challenging yourself to grow—your journey doesn't end here!

As you move forward, keep these practices in mind to make assertiveness a lasting part of your life. With persistence and self-awareness, you can continue to communicate confidently, respect your needs, and nurture healthier relationships.

Reflection: Take a Moment to Look Back

You have reached the end of this book; congratulations! This is an excellent time to consider how far you've come since starting this journey. Here are some questions to help you:

1. **What small steps have you taken lately?**
   Think about times you've put yourself first, spoken

up or set a boundary and said "no," asked for space, or asserted your needs. These moments count, even if they seem minor.

2. **What changes have you noticed in your life?** Are you feeling any shifts? Maybe less stress, more confidence, or more respect from others? Each change matters.

3. **How have these choices made a difference?** Think about any challenging moments you've addressed successfully. Recognizing these shows your growth.

4. **What's one thing you feel proud of?** It could be a boundary you set, a time you spoke up, or simply feeling okay with putting yourself first.

Progress doesn't always shout—it grows quietly, choice by choice. Think back to those small but brave moments where you chose to listen to yourself, stood firm in your needs, or set a boundary you once felt unable to hold. They might seem like ripples, but together, they create real change.

These moments are where the real courage lives. Each time you decided to honor your own voice, each time you let go of guilt and put yourself first, you laid another stone on the path to a life shaped by respect and inner peace. This journey isn't easy, but the strength you've shown, even in the smallest steps, is something to be truly proud of.

So, as you close this book, pause to feel what you've

achieved. Picture the person you're becoming—someone rooted in self-worth and compassion. These choices, these steps, are building the life you've always deserved.

You're further along than you think. Take this with you: You're worthy of every bit of the peace, respect, and happiness that comes from choosing to stand tall.

"Every great dream begins with a dreamer. Always remember, you have within you the strength, the patience, and the passion to reach for the stars to change the world." Harriet Tubman

Appendices

Appendix 1: Daily Interaction Log Template

Date:

Time:

Location:

People Involved:

Person 1:

Person 2:

Others:

Type of Interaction (e.g., Work Meeting, Casual Conversation, Disagreement, etc.):

Description of the Situation:

(Briefly describe the context and content of the interaction.)

My Initial Response:

(Describe your initial emotional and verbal response.)

Assertiveness Level (Passive, Assertive, Aggressive):

The outcome of the Interaction:

(Describe the outcome of the interaction. Was it resolved? Was there a conflict?)

Reflection:

(Reflect on how you handled the interaction. What could have been improved? What did you do well? How could assertiveness have changed the outcome?)

Action Steps for Improvement:

(Based on today's interaction, list any specific actions you can take to improve your assertiveness in future interactions.)

Note: This log template is structured to encourage detailed observation and reflection. It will help you consciously think about how you communicate in different situations and how you might enhance your assertiveness for better outcomes. You may print multiple copies of this log or adapt it into a digital format to use daily.

Appendix 2: Mental Rehearsal Script

Purpose: This mental rehearsal is designed to help you practice and internalize assertive communication. By visualizing yourself in a scenario where assertiveness is needed, you can build confidence and prepare for real-life situations.

Instructions: Find a quiet place where you won't be disturbed. Sit or lie down in a comfortable position. Close your eyes, take a few deep breaths, and begin the mental rehearsal.

Script:

Start by bringing your attention to your breath. Inhale deeply through your nose, filling your lungs completely. Hold the breath for a moment, and then exhale slowly through your mouth, releasing any tension or stress. Take a few more deep breaths, allowing yourself to relax fully into this moment.

Now, imagine that you're in a safe and supportive environment. It might be a cozy room with soft lighting, a counseling office where you feel heard and understood, or even a peaceful spot in nature where you feel completely at ease. This is your space—a place where you can express yourself freely and confidently.

In this safe space, you're finally ready to talk about something that's been bothering you for a while. Picture the situation clearly in your mind. Perhaps it's an issue at work—a project that's causing you stress because of unclear expectations, or maybe it's a recurring conflict with a loved one that has left you feeling unheard and frustrated.

As you focus on this situation, imagine that the person involved is sitting across from you, ready to listen. You feel calm and composed. You know that this is your opportunity to be assertive, to express your thoughts, feelings, and needs directly and honestly.

Now, visualize yourself speaking. Your voice is steady and clear. You're not holding back, but you're also not lashing out. You say exactly what you need to say, using language that is both honest and respectful. For example, you might say, "I've been feeling overwhelmed with the workload lately, and I need clearer guidelines to manage my tasks effectively," or "When we argue, I feel like my perspective isn't being heard, and I'd like us to work on finding a way to communicate better."

As you express yourself, notice how the other person reacts. In your mind, they're listening intently, acknowledging your feelings and your needs. They might not agree with everything you say, but they're open to understanding your perspective. The conversation is productive, leading to a sense of mutual respect and a clearer path forward.

You continue to speak assertively, standing on equal ground with the other person. You respect your own needs and ideas enough to bring them to the table, and you respect theirs enough to listen to what they have to say. There's no need to dominate the conversation or retreat into silence. You're simply communicating your truth in a way that opens the door to understanding.

Take a moment to feel the empowerment that comes from being assertive. Notice the sense of relief that washes over you as you express yourself honestly and directly. You're not aiming to win or lose—you're aiming for a balanced and respectful exchange where everyone's voice is valued.

As you bring this mental rehearsal to a close, take a few more deep breaths. Inhale confidence, and exhale any remaining tension. When you're ready, slowly open your eyes, bringing with you the clarity and calmness you experienced during this exercise.

Remember, assertiveness is a skill that can be practiced and refined. Each time you engage in this mental rehearsal, you're building the confidence and presence of mind to express yourself assertively in real-life situations.

Appendix 3: Achievements Log Template

Instructions: Use this log daily to note down any achievements, big or small. This helps track your progress and reminds you of the positive steps you're taking. Reflecting on what you've accomplished can build confidence and keep you motivated.

Date:

1. **Today's Achievement(s):**
2. **Challenges Overcome:**
3. **How I Felt About My Progress:**
4. **What I Learned Today:**
5. **Positive Reinforcement or Affirmation for Tomorrow:**
    - "I am capable of…"
    - "I am proud of…"

Repeat this daily or weekly, and over time, review your entries to see how far you've come.

Appendix 4: Practical Conversation Starters

Use these conversation starters to express yourself clearly and confidently. Adapt them to fit your voice and situation. Remember, assertiveness respects both your needs and others'. With practice, these phrases will become second nature!

---

1. Setting Boundaries at Work
   - **With a Manager on Overload**:
     "I want to make sure I'm providing my best work. With the current tasks I have, adding another may stretch me thin. Could we prioritize my workload or discuss redistributing some tasks?"

   - **With a Colleague on Interruptions**:
     "I appreciate your input, and I want to give it my full attention. Can we schedule a time later to go over this so I can focus on it properly?"

   - **Regarding Unpaid Overtime**:
     "I've noticed that my work hours have extended beyond the agreed schedule. I'd like to ensure we're sticking to the planned hours to keep a healthy work-life balance."

2. Saying No to Social Invitations
   - **Turning Down an Invitation**:
     "Thank you for the invite! I'll have to pass this time, but please keep me in the loop for future get-togethers."

- **Setting Boundaries with Friends**:
  "I love spending time together, but I need some downtime this weekend. Let's catch up next week instead."

3. Managing Expectations with Family

- **When Family Asks for More Than You Can Give**:
  "I'd love to help, but I'm balancing a lot right now. How about I assist with [specific task] instead?"

- **Setting Boundaries with Parents**:
  "I appreciate your concern and advice. It means a lot to me, but I'd like to handle this in my own way. I'll reach out if I need guidance."

- **Declining to Host a Family Gathering**:
  "I know how much we all enjoy gathering together. This time, though, I'll need to sit out as the host. Perhaps we can rotate hosting or consider a simpler plan?"

4. Clarifying Roles and Responsibilities

- **In a Team Meeting**:
  "To ensure we're all on the same page, could we clarify who will be responsible for each task? I want to make sure I'm contributing effectively and not overlapping with others."

- **On Miscommunication in Tasks**:
  "It seems there was a misunderstanding about who would handle this. To avoid this in the future, can we go over roles together?"

5. Expressing Needs in Relationships

- **Asking for More Support:**
  "I've been feeling a bit overwhelmed and could really use your support with [specific task or emotion]. Could we talk about how we might manage this together?"

- **Addressing Communication Preferences:**
  "I feel more connected when we have uninterrupted time to talk. Could we set aside some time each week to check in with each other?"

- **Discussing Personal Space:**
  "I love spending time with you, and I also need some alone time to recharge. Can we talk about how to balance both?"

6. Handling Conflict Assertively

- **Addressing a Disagreement Calmly:**
  "I understand where you're coming from. I have a slightly different view, and I'd love for us to discuss it to reach a shared understanding."

- **When Receiving Negative Feedback:**
  "I hear your concerns, and I want to improve. Could you give me specific examples so I can work on those areas?"

- **Offering Constructive Feedback:**
  "I value the work you're doing and wanted to share some thoughts on how we might make it even stronger. Would you be open to hearing my feedback?"

7. Asking for What You Want in a Professional Setting

- **Requesting Feedback on Your Work:**
  "I'm focused on my professional growth and would love to get

some feedback on my recent work. Could we set up a time to discuss this?"

- **Seeking a Promotion or New Opportunity:**
  "I've enjoyed taking on responsibilities here and believe I'm ready for the next step. Could we discuss possible paths forward?"

- **Asking for a Raise:**
  "I've been reflecting on my contributions and the value I bring to our team. I'd like to discuss my compensation and explore options for growth."

8. Reclaiming Personal Time

- **Politely Declining Extra Work:**
  "I'm committed to meeting my current deadlines, so I won't be able to take on additional work right now. Could we re-evaluate priorities if necessary?"

- **Setting Boundaries for Unscheduled Requests:**
  "I'm currently focused on another project, so I won't be able to address this right now. Could we plan for it at a later date?"

These conversation starters are intended to help you frame responses respectfully, ensuring clarity without over-explanation.

Appendix 5: Refusal Phrases

Use these refusal phrases as examples for respectfully declining requests or invitations. They can be adapted to suit different situations, helping you protect your time and energy while staying considerate of others. Remember, saying "no" doesn't have to feel harsh; it's about communicating your boundaries in a way that's clear and kind.

---

1. Declining Social Invitations

- *"Thanks for inviting me! I can't make it this time, but let's catch up soon."*

- *"I'd love to join, but I already have plans. Maybe next time?"*

- *"That sounds fun, but I need a quiet evening to recharge. Have a great time!"*

2. Turning Down Additional Work Requests

- *"I'm focused on a few other projects right now, so I won't be able to take on more at the moment."*

- *"I'd love to help out, but my current workload won't allow it. Let's revisit this later if time frees up."*

- *"I want to make sure I can give my best to my existing tasks, so I'll have to say no to any extras right now."*

3. Refusing Unwanted Advice

- *"I appreciate the suggestion! I'd like to try handling it my way, but I'll keep this in mind."*

- *"Thanks for the input. I'm comfortable with the direction I'm going in right now."*
- *"I appreciate your concern, but I'm confident in the approach I'm taking."*

4. Saying No to Volunteering or Committee Requests

- *"I really support what you're doing, but I'm focusing on other commitments at the moment."*
- *"I appreciate the opportunity, but I won't be able to commit this time."*
- *"That's a great cause! Unfortunately, I have to sit this one out, but I'd be happy to help in other ways if possible."*

5. Declining a Request for a Favor

- *"I'd love to help out, but I'm not able to right now."*
- *"Unfortunately, I won't be able to do that, but I hope it goes well for you."*
- *"I'm sorry, but my schedule is tight, and I won't be able to take that on."*

6. Refusing Financial Requests

- *"I'm not in a position to lend any money, but I hope you find the support you need."*
- *"I'm focusing on my own financial goals right now, so I'll have to pass on this."*
- *"I'm unable to contribute financially, but please keep me posted on other ways I might be able to help."*

7. Politely Refusing to Share Personal Information

- *"I'd rather not discuss that, but thanks for understanding."*
- *"I keep those details private, but thanks for asking."*
- *"That's not something I share, but I appreciate your curiosity."*

These refusal phrases offer you flexible, respectful ways to set boundaries and maintain a positive tone.

Appendix 6: Examples of "I" Statements

Use these "I" statements as a guide for expressing your thoughts, feelings, and needs in a clear and respectful way for various situations.

---

1. Expressing Feelings in Personal Relationships

- **When Feeling Unheard**:
  "I feel frustrated when I'm interrupted because I don't get a chance to fully express my thoughts."

- **When Needing More Support**:
  "I feel overwhelmed with everything I have going on right now, and I'd appreciate any help you can offer."

- **Setting a Boundary for Alone Time**:
  "I need some quiet time in the evenings to recharge. It helps me stay balanced and present."

2. Addressing Issues at Work

- **Clarifying Workload with a Manager**:
  "I'm concerned that my current workload may affect the quality of my work. Could we prioritize tasks together to ensure the best results?"

- **Requesting Feedback from a Colleague**:
  "I'd like to improve my work, and I value your insights. Could you share specific feedback on my recent project?"

- **Expressing a Need for Clearer Instructions**:

"I feel more confident in my work when I have clear instructions. Could we go over the details together to make sure I'm on the right track?"

3. Handling Conflicts or Disagreements

- **Expressing a Different Opinion Respectfully**:
  "I see it a little differently. I feel that [share your perspective], and I'd like us to consider both viewpoints."

- **When Feeling Dismissed in a Conversation**:
  "I feel disregarded when my ideas aren't acknowledged, and it's important to me to contribute to this discussion."

- **Addressing Tension in a Group Setting**:
  "I sense there's some tension in our team, and I think it's affecting our work. I'd like us to have an open conversation so we can work through it."

4. Setting Boundaries with Friends or Family

- **When Feeling Overloaded by Requests**:
  "I feel stretched thin with everything on my plate, so I won't be able to help with that right now."

- **Asserting Privacy with Family Members**:
  "I feel more comfortable when certain topics stay private. I'd appreciate it if we could avoid discussing that area."

- **Saying No to a Favor Politely**:
  "I'd love to help, but I'm focusing on other priorities at the moment. I'll let you know if I have more time later."

5. Communicating Needs in Social Situations

- **When Needing a Break from Socializing**:

"I enjoy spending time with everyone, but I feel a bit drained right now. I'm going to step out for a bit to recharge."

- **When Feeling Uncomfortable with Group Decisions**:
  "I feel uneasy about this plan and would prefer something different. Could we discuss some other options?"

- **Expressing a Need to Leave an Event Early**:
  "I had a great time, but I'm feeling tired and need to head home to rest. Thanks for understanding."

6. Addressing Conflicts in Romantic Relationships

- **Expressing Hurt Feelings**:
  "I feel hurt when my opinions aren't considered, and I'd like to work on making decisions together."

- **Requesting Quality Time Together**:
  "I miss spending time together, and I'd love to plan a day where we can focus on each other."

- **Addressing a Recurring Issue**:
  "I feel frustrated when we revisit this issue without resolution. I'd like us to find a way to address it more effectively."

These "I" statements help you voice your concerns, needs, and feelings while keeping the focus on your own experiences rather than pointing fingers.

Appendix 7: Daily Thought Log

Developing assertive communication often means challenging old thought patterns and practicing new ones. A Daily Thought Log is a powerful tool for tracking thoughts and understanding how they impact your feelings and actions. It helps you recognize unhelpful patterns and replace them with assertive alternatives. By regularly using this log, you can make conscious choices in your responses instead of reacting automatically. Take a few minutes each day, or after a challenging interaction, to fill it out.

How to Use the Daily Thought Log

1. **Situation**: Briefly describe the situation that triggered your thought. Be specific, including who was involved and what happened. This provides context for understanding the thought in question.

2. **Automatic Thought**: Write down the immediate thought that went through your mind in response to the situation. This is often a reflexive reaction, such as "I don't want to cause conflict" or "If I say no, they'll be upset."

3. **Emotion**: Record how this thought made you feel. Were you anxious, guilty, frustrated, or perhaps relieved? Rate the intensity of the emotion on a scale of 1–10 to help you gauge the impact of this thought.

4. **Behavior/Response**: Note what you did or didn't

do because of this thought. Did you agree to something against your wishes? Did you avoid expressing yourself or stay silent?

5. **Alternative Thought**: Reflect on whether there's a more balanced, realistic way to interpret the situation. Write down a thought that supports assertive action, such as "It's okay to say no without feeling guilty" or "Expressing my needs respectfully won't ruin the relationship."

6. **New Emotion**: Imagine how the alternative thought makes you feel. This helps reinforce the idea that assertive thoughts can reduce anxiety and promote a sense of control and confidence.

Sample Daily Thought Log Entry

Situation	Automatic Thought	Emotion	Behavior/Response	Alternative Thought	New Emotion
My manager asked me to take on an extra task I don't have time for.	"If I say no, they'll think I'm not committed."	Anxious (8/10)	Agreed to the task, even though I felt overwhelmed	"It's okay to explain my current workload and suggest an alternative."	Relieved (5/10)
Friend asked me to attend an event I'm not interested in.	"If I say no, they'll be disappointed in me."	Guilty (7/10)	Agreed to go despite wanting to decline	"It's okay to have boundaries; I can suggest meeting another time."	Calm (6/10)

Try It: Completing Your Daily Thought Log

Use this log daily or as often as you can when you experience a challenging thought. By tracking your thoughts and responses regularly, you'll become more aware of patterns in your thinking and behavior that may be keeping you from assertive action. Over time, these alternative thoughts will feel more natural, and you'll find it easier to respond assertively in situations where you previously felt pressured or overwhelmed.

Tips for Success:

- **Consistency is Key**: The more frequently you use the log, the more you'll gain insight into your thought patterns.

- **Be Patient with Yourself**: Changing automatic thoughts takes time, so treat each entry as a learning experience.

- **Celebrate Small Wins**: Even minor shifts in thought or behavior are steps toward becoming more assertive. Recognize and celebrate these small successes.

Using the Daily Thought Log over time will empower you to face interactions with clarity and confidence, helping you assert your needs and boundaries naturally and without guilt.

You may keep your Daily Thought Logs in a notebook or journal. By regularly reviewing your entries, you can track progress, notice shifts in your thinking, and build assertive habits that reinforce your self-respect and emotional well-being.

Appendix 8: Examples of Constructive Feedback

Note: This appendix provides a selection of statements designed to help you address undermining behavior calmly and assertively. Each example focuses on describing the behavior and its impact while inviting a more respectful interaction. When using these statements, feel free to adjust the language to suit your style and the specific situation. By addressing issues in a clear, non-confrontational way, you can open the door to constructive, positive change in your interactions.

1. "I noticed that during the meeting, you rephrased my point without acknowledging it was my idea. When this happens, it can feel like my input isn't valued. Moving forward, I'd appreciate if you could acknowledge contributions directly."

2. "When you questioned my decision in front of the team without discussing it with me first, it left me feeling undermined. I'm open to feedback, and it would be helpful if we could discuss any concerns one-on-one beforehand."

3. "When you interrupt me or talk over me during discussions, it can feel as though my perspective is not respected. I'd appreciate being able to finish my thoughts before we move on to new points."

4. "When you speak over my contributions or change direction without input, it gives the impression that my ideas aren't valued. I'd appreciate if we could

collaborate in a way that acknowledges each perspective."

5. "I've noticed you sometimes critique my decisions publicly rather than sharing feedback privately. This approach affects my confidence in presenting ideas. It would be helpful if we could address any concerns directly in private."

6. "When feedback about my work is shared indirectly or through others rather than directly with me, it makes it harder to improve and feels discouraging. I'd appreciate direct communication so I can address any concerns effectively."

7. "I noticed that decisions I've made are sometimes changed without involving me in the discussion. Being left out of these conversations can make me feel undermined. I'd like to be part of these discussions moving forward so we can make informed choices together."

8. "When my suggestions are dismissed without consideration, it feels as though my contributions aren't valued. I'd appreciate if we could explore all ideas on the table, as this helps foster a collaborative environment."

9. "I've noticed that my work is sometimes attributed to others or overlooked. When this happens, it makes me feel undervalued. Moving forward, it

would mean a lot if my efforts could be acknowledged directly."

10. "When my opinions are downplayed or dismissed, it impacts my ability to contribute confidently. I'd like us to work in a way where all perspectives are considered before making decisions, so everyone feels valued."

Appendix 9: Confident Communication

Note: This appendix provides examples of statements you can use to communicate clear next steps when facing recurring issues. These phrases are designed to assert your preparedness to take action if necessary, while maintaining a calm and professional tone. By expressing a willingness to address unresolved matters constructively, you set boundaries and reinforce your commitment to a respectful working environment. Feel free to adapt these statements to suit your specific context.

1. "If this continues, I'll need to bring it up with our team leader to ensure we can address it properly. I'm hoping we can find a solution here together."

2. "Going forward, if we're unable to resolve this directly, I'll explore other options to make sure everyone's contributions are acknowledged."

3. "If the situation persists, I'll need to document this for future reference, as it's important for me to maintain clarity on the steps we're taking to improve."

4. "I'm open to working on this collaboratively, but if we can't reach a solution, I may need to involve HR to discuss how best to handle it moving forward."

5. "If I notice a pattern of this behavior continuing, I'll plan to revisit our conversation with a clear action plan so that we can address it constructively."

6. "If we're unable to resolve this here, I'll look into formal channels to make sure we're all aligned on expectations moving forward."

7. "Should this continue, I'll take the necessary steps to escalate the matter through the proper channels. My goal is simply to ensure we're working effectively together."

8. "If I see that the behavior persists, I'll need to set up a follow-up meeting to discuss this with more detailed action items."

9. "While I hope we can find a solution ourselves, I'm prepared to involve senior management to help mediate if needed."

10. "If we can't settle this collaboratively, I'll consider documenting these instances to ensure there's a record of our efforts to resolve things constructively."

Appendix 10: Bibliography

Author	Title	Publisher	Year of Publication
Paterson, Randy J.	The Assertiveness Workbook	New Harbinger Publications	2000
Smith, Manuel J.	When I Say No, I Feel Guilty	Bantam Books	1975
Brown, Brené	Daring Greatly	Avery	2012
Patterson, Kerry, et al.	Crucial Conversations: Tools for Talking When Stakes Are High	McGraw-Hill Education	2002
Harris, Russ	The Confidence Gap: A Guide to Overcoming Fear and Self-Doubt	Trumpeter	2011
Rosenber, Marshall B.	Nonviolent Communication: A Language of Life	PuddleDancer Press	2003
Covey, Stephen R.	The 7 Habits of Highly Effective People	Free Press	1989
Goleman, Daniel	Emotional Intelligence	Bantam Books	1995

| Pease, Allan, and Barbara Pease | The Definitive Book of Body Language | Bantam Books | 2006 |
| Carnegie, Dale | How to Win Friends and Influence People | Simon & Schuster | 1936 |

Appendix 11: Glossary of Terms

Active Listening
A communication technique that involves fully concentrating, understanding, responding, and remembering what the speaker is saying. It is an essential skill for building trust and fostering clear communication.

Aggressive Communication
A style of communication characterized by expressing one's own needs and desires forcefully, often without consideration for the needs of others. This approach can lead to conflict and strained relationships.

Assertiveness
The ability to express oneself openly and respectfully, standing up for one's own rights while respecting the rights of others. Assertiveness balances confidence and consideration for others' perspectives.

Boundaries
Personal limits or rules that define acceptable behaviors, relationships, and interactions. Setting boundaries is a key element of assertive behavior, protecting one's well-being while fostering respect in relationships.

Catastrophizing
A cognitive distortion that leads individuals to assume the worst possible outcome will occur, often exaggerating the significance or likelihood of negative events.

Cognitive Restructuring

A therapeutic process used to identify, challenge, and change negative thought patterns that contribute to emotional distress. This technique is frequently employed in Cognitive Behavioral Therapy (CBT).

Conflict Resolution

The process of addressing and resolving disagreements or disputes in a way that respects all parties involved. Effective conflict resolution often involves assertive communication, negotiation, and problem-solving skills.

Constructive Feedback

Feedback that focuses on helping an individual improve or develop, delivered in a respectful and supportive manner. Constructive feedback emphasizes actionable suggestions and avoids personal attacks.

Emotional Resilience

The ability to adapt to and recover from difficult situations, stress, or adversity. Emotional resilience supports mental well-being and helps individuals maintain a positive outlook even in challenging times.

Eye Contact

The act of looking directly into another person's eyes during communication. Maintaining appropriate eye contact can convey confidence, attentiveness, and sincerity.

"I" Statements

A communication tool that allows individuals to express their feelings, needs, and perspectives without blaming others. "I" statements promote constructive dialogue and help reduce defensiveness.

Mindfulness

A state of active, open attention to the present moment. Practicing mindfulness can enhance self-awareness, reduce stress, and improve emotional regulation.

Nonverbal Communication

The transmission of messages or signals without words. Nonverbal cues include body language, facial expressions, gestures, posture, and eye contact, all of which play a crucial role in assertive communication.

Passive Communication

A style of communication in which individuals avoid expressing their thoughts, needs, or desires, often out of fear of conflict or rejection. This approach can lead to frustration and feelings of being overlooked.

People-Pleasing

A behavior pattern characterized by prioritizing others' needs and desires at the expense of one's own well-being, often to gain approval or avoid conflict.

Personal Space

The physical area surrounding an individual that they consider their own. Respecting personal space is important for fostering comfortable and respectful interactions.

Reflective Listening

A communication technique in which the listener paraphrases or restates what the speaker has said to demonstrate understanding and foster connection.

Self-Advocacy

The act of expressing one's needs, preferences, and rights effectively, often in situations where support or accommodations are needed.

Self-Worth

A person's intrinsic sense of their own value and worthiness, independent of external validation or success. Building self-worth is often a key aspect of developing assertiveness.

Setting Boundaries

The act of establishing clear limits on what one is willing to accept from others in terms of behavior, demands, or interactions. Setting boundaries is essential for protecting one's well-being and maintaining respectful relationships.

Social Cues

The verbal and nonverbal signals that guide interactions in social settings. Understanding and responding to social cues is important for effective communication and relationship-building.

About the Author

Dr. MG Lazarus has dedicated more than three decades to supporting individuals in their journey to mental wellness and personal growth. His diverse roles as a counselor, social worker, and Catholic Deacon allow him to connect on multiple levels, offering not only practical solutions but also compassionate understanding. With advanced studies in Social Work, Philosophy, Theology, and Management, as well as a Ph.D., Dr. Lazarus brings both depth and breadth to his approach, blending evidence-based strategies with genuine care.

In *Break Free to Own Your Space*, Dr. Lazarus draws on years of experience to help readers break free from the pressures of pleasing others. His work emphasizes building confidence, expressing needs clearly, and maintaining healthy relationships. The book is designed to be a practical guide, offering step-by-step advice on overcoming common barriers to assertiveness.

Additional Works by Dr. MG Lazarus:

- *From Tears to Tranquillity: Finding Strength After Loss*

  This compassionate guide supports those grappling with grief, offering insight and actionable steps to find resilience and renewed hope after loss.

- *Do You Say YES When You Want to Say NO: Learn*

the Art of Assertiveness Step by Step.

Focused on empowering readers, this book teaches assertive communication techniques, helping individuals stand firm in their boundaries and live authentically.

www.ingramcontent.com/pod-product-compliance
Ingram Content Group UK Ltd.
Pitfield, Milton Keynes, MK11 3LW, UK
UKHW020054191224
452586UK00009B/258